You, Free

FIFTY ELEGANT LESSONS IN FREEDOM

CHARLOTTE OSTERMANN

MotherheartPress

ISBN-13: 978-1-7321037-0-2

Table of Contents

"IF YOU WANT TO TEACH PEOPLE A NEW WAY OF THINKING, DON'T BOTHER TO TEACH THEM. INSTEAD, GIVE THEM A TOOL, THE USE OF WHICH WILL LEAD TO NEW WAYS OF THINKING."

BUCKY FULLER

Introduction

ABOUT FREEDOM

Freedom is easier than it looks, and harder than it seems!

Because it is not a steady state, or a final point of accomplishment, we move in the always-shifting interior landscape without a fixed point of reference. Or, rather, our reference is to our own experience of freedom. We return, over and over to the subjective experience of freedom, moving toward that 'sweet spot' from every direction in which we have taken missteps into un-freedom.

Here are some things you should know about freedom before you begin this book:

1 | FREEDOM IS POSSIBLE

If you hold to any belief system that denies the possibility of human freedom, we have a problem. If you are not truly free in the exercise of your will, why bother? What will be will be, and whatever fate, or your genes, or your conditioning has determined you will do, you'll do it. If you will keep reading in spite of any doubts about whether freedom is possible, you'll become more free immediately.

2 | FREEDOM STARTS IN YOU

Given the possibility of human freedom in general, you may still wonder whether your particular freedom (from addiction, from poverty, from prison, from whatever restricts or impedes or compromises you) is possible. I assure you that YOU, personally and particularly, may possess a full and glorious interior freedom despite every challenge you face! That glorious freedom will transform the systems and situations that limit you, from within You, Free.

3 | BECOMING FREE IS RISKY BUSINESS

The greater your freedom, the more you challenge the systems and structures, the norms and patterns of those around you. Your presence may threaten others, because you, yourself, become an invitation to freedom. Many people would rather stay locked in 'safe' and predictable behavior patterns than risk reaching out for the full development of their own freedom. Moving toward freedom may feel scary to you, too, as it does call for you to release your habitual self-defense patterns.

4 | FREEDOM IS JOYFUL

Think of the dancer who, after years of practice, executes her movements with ease and perfection. Freedom of movement becomes joy-in-motion. The same is true for You, Free. Your freedom, fully realized, becomes joy-in-being. You'll learn to scan yourself for the ease, the delight, the joy, and the clarity freedom brings to your actions, then to recover more and more quickly when you notice the symptoms of un-freedom.

5 | FREEDOM INCREASES AS YOU EXERCISE IT

Every free response to the realities you encounter will increase your capacity for freedom. Just as a muscle being used increases in power, you will increase in response-ability as you act, freely. You're going to love this!

Now, if you believe freedom is possible, delightful, and worth the risk of not fitting in with people who prefer the safe limits of the status quo, let's move on.

What does *You, Free* look like? Like this:

Let me show you!

ABOUT FoAm

That simple triangle-circle ($\triangle$) is the basis of the 'language' in which this book is written. That language is called ***FoAm***, and you can read more about its development in the appendix. For now, it is enough to know that it is an 'elegant solution' to the complex problem of addressing the intensely personal and varied dynamics of Self. The term 'elegance' is used by scientists and mathematicians to describe a "unique combination of surprising power and uncommon simplicity."

You, Free is a way of speaking about the interiority and freedom of the human person in an easily understood symbolic 'language'. These easy-to-draw symbols give us a certain cognitive distance from issues that can cause tremendous emotional interference, and also give us metaphoric access to deep dynamics of our mental maps, physical-emotional content, historical subtext and other non-verbal information. FoAm is, thus, something like an 'algebra of personhood' that allows free play with symbols that correspond to otherwise distant and unwieldy realities.

I have found that this symbology, this conversation, is very accessible for men, women, young and old, people without much patience with self-help books and people who have not spent much time in self-discovery. It has the flexibility to adapt to their subjective experience, while giving them a means of communicating about that experience with a light touch – and even with humor. When friends or spouses speak in FoAm together, it becomes a tool for greater understanding of and better communication about relationships and family dynamics.

HOW TO READ THIS BOOK

Ideally, you will open this book in conversation with someone else. The 'grammar' of this new language is learnable in mere minutes. Relating it to your own experience, and conveying that experience in the new terms will give you the most benefit.

This is a workbook, with lots of free space for your own jottings. No skill at drawing is needed to reproduce FoAm in your journal, on the back of napkins, in the margins of books, or in the dirt. Believe me, you'll start finding applications for it everywhere!

Begin with Lesson 1, then go forward in order, or skip around. There are many cross-references between lessons, and a topical index to help you find relationships between them. No matter in what order you read, early lessons will yield new lessons when re-read after others. The simplification you see is the end result of long experience using FoAm and discovering its potential. My prayer is that it will open to disclose that depth of insight to you as you read, re-read, and work with the language in writing and in conversation.

RESPOND

You are invited, after every lesson, to stop and respond. Please take that seriously, as your freedom grows by every response – by every act of freedom. Skipping that step undermines the entire Practice, but you are free to skip it! Surely, by the time you've read through once, you'll better understand why it is *by responding* that you become fully free.

Your response – your act of freedom – looks like this: ⟁
Let me show you!

"BETWEEN STIMULUS AND RESPONSE THERE IS A SPACE. IN THAT SPACE IS OUR POWER TO CHOOSE OUR RESPONSE. IN OUR RESPONSE LIES OUR GROWTH AND OUR FREEDOM."

VIKTOR E. FRANKL

I. Beginning Being Free

Will You Be Free?

This is a person:

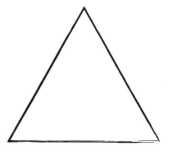

Freedom looks like this:

This is You, Free:

Here are some people who are not free:

People who aren't free are buried under life,

        trapped or imprisoned,

                stretched too thin,

                        displaced, unprotected,

                                afraid to be,

                                        filled with darkness.

WHEN YOU SEE THE STOP SIGN, TAKE A MOMENT TO CONSIDER THE INVITATION TO FREEDOM. RESPOND, TO CREATE YOUR FREEDOM.

There are many ways to be un-free. The good news is that as you respond in freedom, you recover your freedom, expand it, enjoy it!

Please, take a minute and reflect on these thoughts. Consider how you have lost freedom, and how you might regain it again.

You are

cordially invited to

be free!

☐ *ACCEPT*

☐ *DECLINE*

Becoming

You *are* – you have **being**.

This **reality** is much more than just the mere fact that you exist.

Imagine holding this tiny shape in your hand:

Imagine it is so heavy you cannot lift its weight.
Being starts small-and-weighty then expands in all directions.

This is **becoming**. You are **becoming** free.

To be more fully free is to be more and more fully YOU! It takes time.

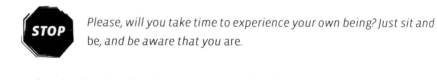

Please, will you take time to experience your own being? Just sit and be, and be aware that you are.

You need a ***place*** to ***be***.

You have your body, a home, and other physical places.

A baby has his mother's womb.

Since ***being*** is not just your body, you need a ***place*** which is much more spacious.

You need a ***person*** – one who will give you space within himself to expand, to unfurl your being.

God is the perfect ***person***, the perfect ***place*** to ***be***.

In Him you will have all the room you need to become ***You, Free***.

All the people in history unfolded within a person, as you have, and as you will continue to do.

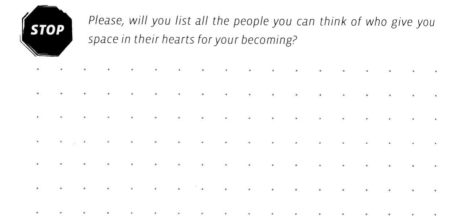

STOP   *Please, will you list all the people you can think of who give you space in their hearts for your becoming?*

To become *You, Free*, you must move toward You, freely.

You might move right past it, but soon you'll find your balance and stay free.

You, Free is You, Here:

Without freedom, you are divided against yourself:

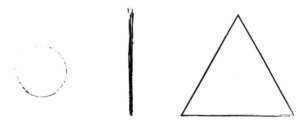

dis-integrated,

     unable to hold yourself together,

         fractured,

            double-minded,

                hiding from yourself.

STOP   *Please, will you list any evidence you've noticed that you are divided against your own being?*

UN–BEING

This person has pulled himself tightly into his own boundary, or been pushed down into a corner, or guarded himself so fully he is imprisoned in his own fort:

This person has run away from limits, or discomfort, or has completely forgotten what he looks like, or has had his boundaries violated, or is seeking the counterfeit peace of un-being:

The further you get from freedom, the more un-being pulls at you.

If keeps going, he will contract his being into such a small space, he will hardly have **being** at all.

If ⬭ keeps going, he will expand his being into such a vast nothingness, he will hardly have **being** at all.

Freedom calls you back to being **You, Free.**

Please, will you write about times when you've experienced these extremes of un-freedom?

Please, will you write about times when you've experienced these extremes of un-freedom?

DISCOMFORT

If you are fractured, it will grow easier and easier to stay small, vague, hidden, unbalanced, dis-integrated.

The road back to **You, Free** grows steeper.

Little problems loom like big walls.

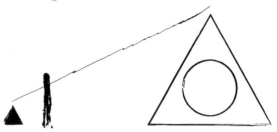

Freedom can seem like a mountain that is too hard to climb. Luckily, you have place in the hearts of others. Your being is distributed so that you don't bear the full weight of dragging yourself back to freedom. Someone goes ahead of you, holding your place for you, carrying some of your stuff, making the trip easier.

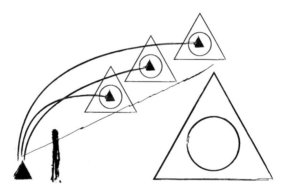

Don't you feel lighter already?

If you are dis-integrated, it will grow harder and harder to make the effort to **move** back to **You, Free**.

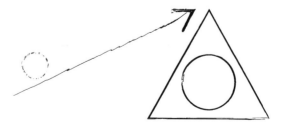

How much easier it feels to roll back down! It might not be free, but collapse makes no demands, takes no effort.

What is it that makes you keep trying, or, at least, keep wishing to be **You, Free**?

You! Your own **being** is fighting for survival!

Inside the tiniest person is a pinprick of the light that wants to open, to expand, to **be**.

Outside the vaguest hint of person is an idea of self that wants to be coherent, respected, articulated, expressed, to **be**.

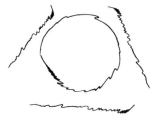

It's actually very, very draining to live in an unfreedom of any kind. Moving toward freedom is worth the discomfort you experience.

STOP *Please, will you list any barrier you can think of to your freedom?*

LINE & SPACE

Suppose you have a space to enclose. It doesn't matter what shape your fence takes, just so you get so-many square inches closed in.

Here is the longest possible line (the most expensive fence!) you could use:

Suppose you have a length of fencing material, and you want to use it to enclose the largest possible space. You don't care what shape your fence takes, just so you get as much space as possible enclosed.

Here is the best shape (the most efficient) to use:

A free person is a ***both-and***: a unity of beauty and efficiency; space and substance; form and emptiness.

YOU, FREE: A simple, spacious FREE-ness draped in an extravagant and complex YOU-ness.

STOP *Please, will you describe the most wonderful, spacious, extravagantly appointed space you can remember, or imagine?*

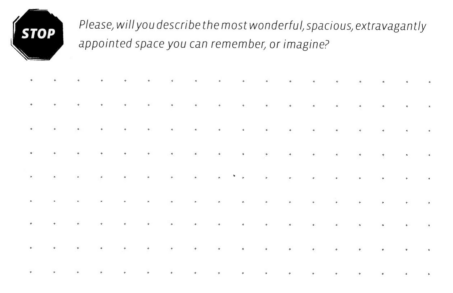

UNFOLDING

It takes years and years for all the YOU-ness of *You, Free* to unfold. Along the way, pieces get lost bent, broken. Some put-together sections are rearranged. You receive new pieces continuously. At some point you see that this is a three-dimensional puzzle – much more complex than you imagined!

All along the way, you are still you, but you aren't fully expressed, fully ***real***-ized.

You, Free is the 'picture on the puzzle box', guiding the unfolding and healing and putting of all your pieces together. God holds that picture in His mind for you. It takes years and years for all the FREE-ness of *You, Free* to expand. Along the way, things clutter the space, curtains fall across the opening, you forget to clean the dust bunnies – the old habits of unfreedom. Now and then you settle for something less than whole, true, glorious freedom.

All along the way, you are still free, but your freedom isn't fully developed, fully ***real***-ized.

You, Free is a vessel full of the largest possible space. The Big Question is what you will put in there?

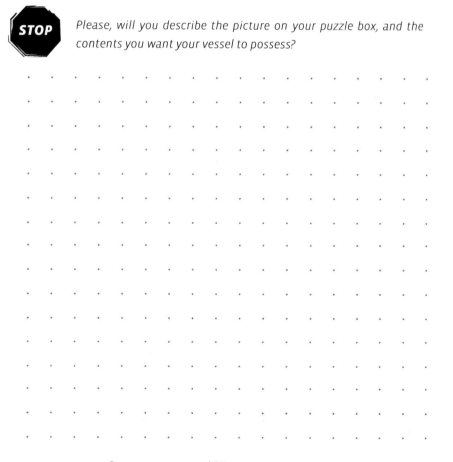

STOP   *Please, will you describe the picture on your puzzle box, and the contents you want your vessel to possess?*

"ONE OF THE ESSENTIAL CONDITIONS OF INTERIOR FREEDOM IS THE ABILITY TO LIVE IN THE PRESENT MOMENT. ...HERE IS THE ONLY PLACE WHERE WE CAN MAKE FREE ACTS. ONLY IN THE PRESENT MOMENT ARE WE TRULY IN CONTACT WITH REALITY."

JACQUES PHILIPPE, *INTERIOR FREEDOM*

II. Your Journey to Freedom

JOURNEY

The journey to **You, Free** starts here, now, and goes on beyond the limit of your imagination.

If you have already begun, you may find yourself swinging back and forth past freedom, to the opposite way of being un-free. Be careful, the magnet of un-being can pull if you swing too far past freedom!

Like a pendulum, your swings should grow smaller over time, until you are at rest.

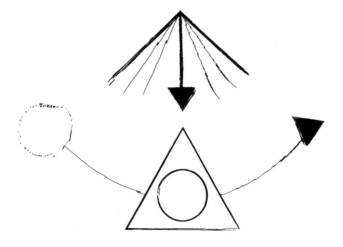

You, Free is You, at rest, centered, still, unmoved by external force or disordered desire, poised to go where you will. Your will remains free unless you freely agree to stay in bondage. When you exercise it, your will grows strong enough to keep you free.

STOP *Please, will you describe a time you've experienced the swinging pendulum?*

ACTION

By acting freely, you become free. This is not the same as pretending to be free! To act freely is to take a step in your own volition, in response to the effect of an encounter with reality, taking into account as much reality as possible.

Be aware which direction you are swinging away from *You, Free*, to figure out what kind of correction you need to stay free.

Do you need tiny, opening steps toward greater generosity, trust, humanity, and beauty?
Or, do you need tiny, limiting steps toward greater definition, clarity, articulation, and boundary?

First, you must attend to your *being*. Whatever reality you face will affect your emotions. Your mind and heart must communicate, and then engage your will, your action, in the work of freedom.

By every act of freedom, you create your freedom.

STOP *Please, will you describe the kinds of things that help you open, and those that help you feel contained, embraced, safe?*

REST

The addict thinks, "I can't help it – I just fall into the old habit." He swings wide, grasping at 'pleasure', to ride its wave without the effort of moving himself.

If he can learn to notice that instant of making the choice, he will grow in freedom. He falls into un-being and feels safe there for a while, but never can be quite at rest, or content, there.

To move yourself freely requires a delicate balance of restraint and risk.

You, Free, instead of riding waves . . .

. . . moves toward freedom, instead of back into the illusion of freedom, or back into slavery. You, Free has rest in the center, instead of paralysis at the edge of being.

STOP *Please, will you describe the deepest rest you have ever known?*

TENSION & COMPRESSION

While you work to become free, part of the reality you must face, and respond to, is the force of compression. Things that push at you, or limit you from the outside, seem to squeeze the breath (and the space) out of you. Money worries, handicaps, the demands of a boss, or child, a messy house, bad weather, living in a war zone, peer pressure, all press down.

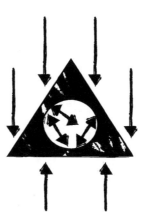

From inside, you feel tensions – impossible paradoxes and simple conflicts between your own desires. Some examples of tension:

> *"I am a mom and a wife and the two roles conflict sometimes; I love you but you hurt me; we live together, but it is hard not to be irritated; he is an artist but wants to honor God; can faith and science contradict?; we need rest and work to live well; I feel very angry, but I want to become a saint; learning a new skill; filthy imaginations plague me; I'm hungry; that hurts!"*

STOP *Please, will you write down some of the tensions and compressions you experience?*

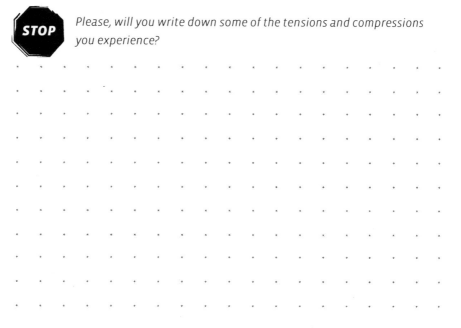

THE ARCH

The architect's answer to the problem of tension and compression is the arch. You see arches supporting great bridges and buildings. They are opening up space with structure, granting freedom through form.

You may have tried to support your fragile being by putting up pillars inside. They really clutter up the place within you!

When you feel pushed down, try opening that space – expanding the arch – instead of toughening up, or filling space with junk pillars and rubble. What was it that helps you open, causes your arch to widen?

When you feel tension from within, try opening that space – expanding the arch. Nothing you shove under the mat, or pretend away, or think you've thrown out really goes away. It stays there kicking your emotions under the table, trying to get your attention. You might react without even knowing why. Very un-free!

Please, will you remember how you reacted to provocation, and write a different way you could have responded?

A window has a frame, and a clear pane. So do you.

But the pane becomes dirty, cracked, steam-clouded. There may be bumper stickers and old pictures and to-do lists and old gunky tape stuck on, too.

The frame may be poorly built, letting in air and snow, keeping the window from opening.

You, Free needs to be transparent, strong, well-housed, beautifully framed, and functioning smoothly to let in the most air, the most light, and to frame the view with integrity.

All the efforts of your being toward these attributes move you toward freedom. All your efforts toward these attributes contribute to You, Free.

You can't go wrong aiming for beauty and transparency and integrity. Beauty has a way of opening doors. Within you, it opens a window to freedom.

STOP *Please, will you write about the things you think are beautiful?*

DESIRE

Here you are:

You are very small. You yearn to become, to grow up.

Something much bigger is attracting you to the world around you. Because your *being* is reaching for that something, you are attracted to everything.

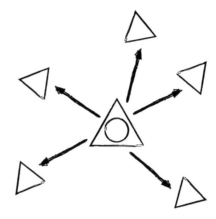

So many things!

You were made to reach out and possess reality.

Your being reaches through everything that is, to the One thing you need most: God, the One who created it all. Things that point to Him satisfy you best, and help you keep going, keep becoming **You, Free**.

Taking everything in causes interior discomfort. Things (even good things) fight against each other, against you. You're losing space. Clear it out, keep some, dump some, work on it. While you are working on it, along comes something big, promising to allay that discomfort effortlessly. Whew!

You grab it, and it does feel as though there's no more problem. One big thing blotted out all that other stuff, but now it weighs you down.

It even grows and demands more space. Everything you take in wants to expand within you, like a seed. You will be very uncomfortable if you ingest something that represents death, destruction, poison, twisted desire, or a lie about reality.

What you take in, you become!

Soon, you're looking for something to take care of this discomfort, and on it goes.

You, Free doesn't stop desiring, but stops fulfilling the desire for the Big Thing with a bunch of lesser things.

STOP *Please, will you list everything you can think of that you 'take in' physically, emotionally, mentally?*

THE BIG THING

The Big Thing you desire is to be You, Free.

So far, so good. You need that desire to cause you to move toward freedom. Why does this end up causing problems?

Your desire to be You, Free didn't originate with you. God planted it there, and wants You, Free even more than you do! Your freedom is to be fulfilled in Him.

He's ahead of you on the road back to the particulars, constraints, duties, pain, reality and smallness of being human. (He has been there, done that, remember?)

In fact, He is the You, Free at the center of all being. He draws you there, carries you there, shows you the path, sends people to help bear your load on the way, holds open a huge place within His own being, His own heart, for You, Free!

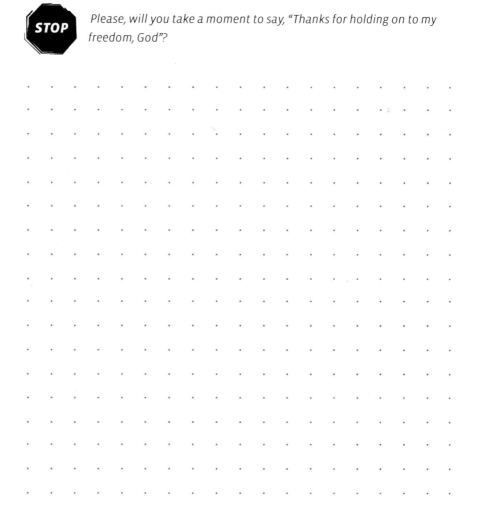

STOP *Please, will you take a moment to say, "Thanks for holding on to my freedom, God"?*

getting closer...

You want to be free, and you want it now!

You feel frustration at the wobbliness and lack of 'progress' you experience. Frustration adds to the interior tension you feel. Your idea of freedom is glorious, but you are much too weak to take more than tiny steps toward it (and too proud to admit the smallness of what you can actually accomplish!)

You are impatient with your own failures, chafing against your limitations, in love with the idea of freedom, but not loving toward your own being. You are dividing yourself further from yourself by fighting against that nasty 'other' within, who seems to cause all your troubles.

Until 'you' get a truce going with 'you', You, Free will be just a vague, un-realized, idea. Love your 'enemy', and work with yourself to restore unity.

STOP *Please, will you write a treaty with yourself – a cease fire, a promise to work together for You, Free?*

APPEARANCES

A person swinging like a pendulum is a little better off than the one who doesn't move toward freedom at all.

You may look wackier, and do more embarrassing things, and throw your life into turmoil, but someone who never moves is increasing his un-freedom every day. At least you're noticing the gap between you and **_You, Free!_** You can't tell by looking whether someone else is free.

You'll know by the effects of freedom: love, joy, peace, patience, kindness, goodness, gentleness, faithfulness, and self-control. Sound familiar? These are the gifts of God, who meets you each time you stop in the center of your pendulum swing and invite Him in. The longer you stay free, the more help His Spirit pours in.

You, Free = an open channel for wisdom and grace to enter the world! You are God's response to the realities you face.

STOP *Please, will you describe what you'd like to help bring into the world?*

"MY FREEDOM WILL BE SO MUCH THE
GREATER AND MORE MEANINGFUL THE
MORE NARROWLY I LIMIT MY FIELD OF
ACTION AND THE MORE I SURROUND MYSELF
WITH OBSTACLES. WHATEVER DIMINISHES
CONSTRAINT DIMINISHES STRENGTH. THE
MORE CONSTRAINT ONE IMPOSES, THE MORE
ONE FREES ONESELF OF THE CHAINS THAT
SHACKLE THE SPIRIT."

IGOR STRAVINSKY

III. Elements of Freedom

LESSON NINETEEN ## EXPANSION

Imagine a hole opening up where you thought your solid Self was secure. Now imagine that hole getting bigger. Your substance seems to be draining away, or breaking apart, or stretching to a snapping point.

Snap! That's the response of a material to too much tension. Growing more spacious, more free, causes tension. Tension isn't all bad! Freedom is finding, not eliminating the Self. Don't worry!

Be gentle. You can't force this upon yourself without violating 'you'. If you fear losing yourself, you might swing to the opposite extreme – and lose yourself there instead.

If you run away from discomfort to the opposite pole of un-being, you are reacting: un-free.

Come back! You are in charge here. No one can force the interior changes you are choosing. They are the work of freedom. Rest here, where you are. Wait until you are free to choose, then do what you want.

STOP *Please, will you write down what you are afraid of?*

CONTRACTION

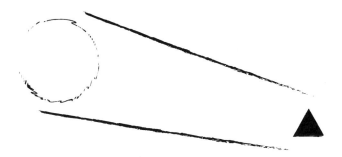

When this person moves toward You, Free, contraction occurs and he holds together better as a vessel, has more 'tone'. He may feel frightened, as though entering a narrow, dark, constricting space.

Imagine entering a dark cave that grows smaller as you proceed inward. As the walls of your being are repaired and strengthened, you may feel they are closing in on you. You may feel your soul is smothering, or being buried alive, or fading away.

Be gentle. You can't force this upon yourself without violating 'you'. In fear of being reduced to nothingness, you might react and leap to the opposite pole of un-being – violating yourself by being reduced to a label, a condition, an anonymous body. Un-free.

STOP *Please, will you write yourself a loving invitation to come home?*

COURAGE

You are about to cross the street. You look both ways. You take in information through your senses. How far is that car? How slick is the street? Is that siren heading this way? How long has that light been red already?

You process information about your own being. How strong does my bad knee feel today? Can I move fast enough while carrying this load?

You notice things without even realizing them. That driver doesn't see me here. The kid is gunning his engine. He's gonna spring as soon as the light turns.

Your life is at stake, yet you make a judgment and act on it, as though you had done this a thousand times! You don't cower in fear on one side of the street. You don't charge headlong into dense traffic. You don't deliberate over your decision endlessly.

You move. In freedom. You, Free. See?

STOP *Please, will you write about the street you need to cross right now? What are the risks, what information do you have? What will you do?*

YOUR BRAIN

You are more than your brain cells and the nerve impulses that electrify you, but your brain is a sort of picture of your being. It looks like this:

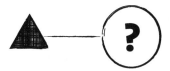

The left side likes small, dense, symbolic packets of meaning. The right side likes big, multifaceted, symbolic networks of meaning. Words, images. Clarity, mystery. You need both. The two are meant to be a unity:

The right side is dependent on the left – the way a child is dependent on a parent, or the way neon requires tubes shaped into letters in order to glow as the words, "All-Night Diner". The capacity of a vessel is a crucial feature, but it is dependent on the form of the vessel for its shape and dimension.

The left side needs the in-formation the right side gains by encounter with reality. The right side needs the organizing principle of words. The left needs material to re-present. Together they create form from ideas.

Together, with good communication, they realize You, Free!

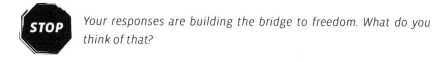

STOP *Your responses are building the bridge to freedom. What do you think of that?*

CORRECTION

Different people need different correctives. As they establish clearer communication with self, they achieve greater integration and wholeness. The bridge to freedom is the connection between the two aspects of your being.

Things that correct toward expansion:

physical relaxation * *exercise that leads to endorphin release and feelings of joy* *uplifting music* * *prayer* * *deep rest* *massage* *sharing thoughts with a friend* *time with nature's beauty* *giving to those in need* *arts and crafts* *dance* *holding a baby* *petting a dog* * *opening a window* * *taking a deep breath*

Things that correct toward contraction:

writing down your thoughts *formal prayers* *physical fitness that leads to muscle tone* * *discipline* *schedules* *filing systems* *organization of the environment* *stating your problems to a counselor* * *keeping a promise* *making an appointment* *fasting* *written rules and policies* *outlining a book*

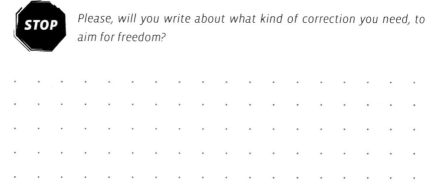

STOP

Please, will you write about what kind of correction you need, to aim for freedom?

FEAR

A note to : If you feel fear, STOP!

Freedom may feel a bit scary to you.

Focus on the image of the largest space you can imagine being in comfortably, and relax there. The image of safe containment should help quell the rising fear that you might lose 'all you have' if you move toward freedom.

Wait until you feel at rest within a place that is not your own mind, your own narrow rut of habit, your own hiding place. Your work is to create and inhabit this imaginary sanctuary. Fill it with light and as much sensory detail as you can. Your imagination can be the opening to **You, Free.**

Fear contracts you. If you guard yourself too closely, you may build walls that will not expand with your new freedom. Your being needs to develop trust in this process. In that private sanctuary within, you can be present to yourself and say, "I promise not to violate you." You can wait for fear to pass. You can ask God to come in and help. He will not violate you either, or come in unless you ask.

STOP *Please, write a description of this place where you are safe.*

REBELLION

A note to ⟳ : If you feel rebellious, STOP!

Coming into order can feel somewhat scary.

Rebellion is sometimes just a reaction to a deeper sense of panic. The big ideas you have about changing yourself may seem to erase your mental image of YOU. The dis-integrated person can feel divided against himself.

Scan your ideas to find the smallest possible movement you can make toward accepting restraint, or the smallest statement you can make to communicate what you need. You will know when your action is just the right-sized step to take when you feel you can take it freely, without resisting.

Your work is to discover tiny, specific steps toward You, Free. They might be so small you feel this will take forever, but you'll be surprised how they add up. The important thing is to act in freedom, and not because you think you have to.

STOP *Please, write about the tiny, even symbolic steps that are possible right now, for real, for you.*

SEEING DOUBLE

Your eyes see two images. Your brain resolves them into one. *You, Free* is two aspects of being resolved into one clear, whole, coherent, free person. There is only one thing there, but seeing it 'double' gives the brain more information, for a more accurate image. You are already one specific, unique, unrepeatable, whole person. YOU are a unity of body, mind, emotions, and will.

You, Free is you, in focus.

The closer you get, the greater you will feel. You will continue to be imperfect, but knowing the sweet spot, the ideal of freedom, will help you approach the top of that mountain. *You, Free* is the most *YOU* and the most *FREE* you can be. *You, Free* looks more and more like 'the real you', and less like the mask you've been wearing.

It is hard to be *YOU* and see *YOU* at the same time. You need to imagine *You, Free* to move toward freedom, but your lack of freedom impairs your ability to imagine.

Lucky for you, God placed someone in your life whose whole job is to hold *You, Free* in mind. Your guardian angel knows *YOU*, and reminds you what *You, Free* is all about.

Others hold your being in their own hearts, but their image of you is affected by their own lack of freedom, of focus, of capacity to imagine. Your guardian angel has no such trouble. He can keep You, Free in mind, no matter how you deform yourself. People who reflect back to you the most clear image of *You, Free* are like guardian angels.

More and more, as you become free, your own imagination will be able to form and hold a coherent sense of You, Free. Until then, ask your guardian angel to help you bear that burden, help you focus.

STOP *Please, will your write about the guardian angels (real angels, and the people who hold you in their hearts) who help you imagine You, Free?*

THE ENEMY

Your enemy is not you, but whoever is lying to you, pushing you toward smallness, or inviting you to have no boundaries.

Your true friend, like your guardian angel, and like God, sees **You, Free** and is sad when you act like someone else. Your un-being gives him pain, because you have a place in his heart.

Your enemy sees your flaws and screw-ups and says, "That's the real you!" Your true friend says, "That's not like you."

Your true friend invites you to freedom. Your enemy invites you to your own unmaking. Maybe he is taking over all the territory you abandon. Maybe he just feels bigger, the smaller you get.

Hmmmm…this time, say NO!

STOP *Please, make a list of people who have an interest in keeping you un-free. If you have any invitations from true friends, please say yes.*

TUG–OF–WAR

Between **YOU MUST!** and **I WILL NOT!** Lies the abyss of **CAN'T**.

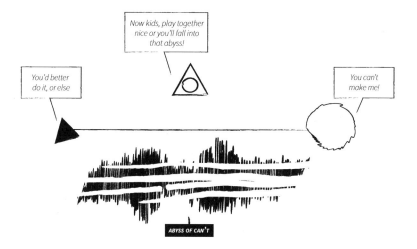

The disintegrated will can become power hungry. Like a slave-driver the will-to-power can push for change, or – like a powerless bully – can exert itself in destructive strength. If you try to whip yourself into shape, you may trigger your own passive resistance. The net result of this war is that, even if some work gets accomplished, freedom does not develop.

Worse, the unexercised capacity for freedom can atrophy and leave you impotent to act without coercion. **You, Free** needs power to act in freedom. This is also known as an internal locus of control, free agency, or self-mastery.

Undisciplined children are sometimes called 'strong willed,' because they resist obedience. In reality, they are weak-willed, because they cannot wield themselves in correspondence with legitimate authority, or with their own best interests. For a child, and for You, Free, the hope is to grow more and more able to call forth acts that 'correspond to Reality, in the totality of its factors' (Fr. Giussani's definition of freedom).

You aim for freedom with a divided mind. You earnestly desire to scale that mountain, but this movement causes new tension, and your 'other half' pulls against your best efforts in fear of upheaval. You seemed to be 'at peace' with yourself the way you were. Now you feel 'at war'. Becoming free places you in a zone of turbulence where there is real tension that is hard to resolve.

As Fulton Sheen said, "Free will is a gift, but freedom is a conquest."

Ally with yourself to conquer and hold the territory of **You, Free**. Make a treaty.

STOP *Please, will you pray for help becoming single-minded and actually write up a peace treaty between the 'triangle' and 'circle' aspects of your own being?*

GOOD JUDGEMENT

There's 'being judgmental' and then there's 'making a good judgement. They are quite different things. To become free, you must make the best possible judgement about what action to take. Your act is free to the extent it is based on good judgement.

Every free act strengthens **_You, Free._**

A Good Judgement looks (surprise!) like a free person:

As Fr. Giussani says, it's a "judgement with heart in it."

Its components are Reason ⟋⟍ and Affect ◯ or "head" and "heart."

Start with the ⟋⟍ factors.

Consider the objective Reality you face:

> *What is external to you? What boundaries, limits, or constraints do you face? Is there any time factor, a demand for action, necessity involved? Look through what you've written to see if there are any terms that need clear definition, or information that must be obtained to clarify the situation.*

Next, look at the ◯ factors.

Consider the subjective Reality you face:

> *What has provoked you? How do you feel about what's happening? Are your feelings proportional to this Reality? If not, what associations are being triggered in this encounter? What do you need in this moment? What do you want?*

Describe the interior dimension, tension, and dynamics of this situation.

Now you have a clearer picture of the internal (subjective) and external (objective) factors of Reality. You can see a tension between them that awaits resolution. The more impossible it seems to resolve them, the more you need the creative help of the Spirit.

Pray for it! Wait for it! Don't act until you have made a Good Judgement about what act will be a response to this reality, and not a reaction. Act! Unrealized ideas are dangerous. They may become Vain Imaginations, releasing the tension without exercising freedom.

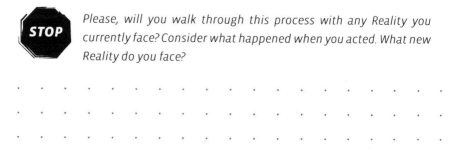

STOP *Please, will you walk through this process with any Reality you currently face? Consider what happened when you acted. What new Reality do you face?*

"IF WE VALUE THE FREEDOM OF MIND AND SOUL, IF WE'RE PARTISANS OF LIBERTY, THEN IT'S OUR PLAIN DUTY TO ESCAPE, AND TO TAKE AS MANY PEOPLE WITH US AS WE CAN!"

J.R.R. TOLKIEN, *ON FAIRY STORIES*

IV. Mountains and Valleys

Falling Heavenward*

If you are running in the path of God's commands, moving ahead, growing and going, running the race, stopping can be the hardest act of all.

Lucky for you, you don't have to choose it. Impediments will stop you cold. You'll be derailed by circumstances beyond your control, thwarted by people beyond your control, interfered with by demons beyond your control, and re-routed by a God beyond your control.

So, how is it a free act if it happens to you passively?

Being stopped calls for you to look deeper for your freedom, deeper for God's guidance, deeper for a way to turn victimhood into newness of life.

As always, Christ abides in you at the core – as the core – of your freedom, guidance, and creativity. The highest freedom is to do freely what you must. And this is where the catenary arch is so helpful.

Catholic architect Antoni Gaudí discovered the catenary is nature's most elegant solution to the material balance of tensive and compressive forces. You can see it by holding up the two ends of a string, or putting on a chain necklace (catena = chain). The gentle curve formed as the supported chain falls freely is a catenary curve. Gaudí turned it upside down and, literally, raised the roof!

When you are thwarted, impeded, stopped, all the 'material' of your forward energy tends to bunch up at that barrier point in mounting frustration and impotence. If (and, the sooner the better!) you can actively stop instead of being passively stopped, and release all that forward-

*THIS LESSON IS COPIED FROM MY BOOK ***DARE YOUR SOMETHING!***

pushing (now a compressive energy, because it has no outlet) and progress-demanding (the new interior tension that is causing frustration because it is powerless to change reality) to Christ, you will experience catenary freedom.

This will likely feel like a falling – a falling back into childlike trust. Simply fall. Let go. Fall heavenward like a catenary arch. It is good for your arch to be made of strong, solid stuff; like a Roman arch;

good for your arch to be buttressed externally, like a Gothic arch,

and good for your arch to distribute all the forces it bears to one single, simple point in the free-fall of perfect surrender. Choose the image you need to fit the reality you face.

WHEN YOUR ARCH IS SMALL, FALL HEAVENWARD...THINK CATENARY...RELEASE IT TO CHRIST, WHO CAN BEAR ALL.

STOP *Please, will you draw a circle with a dot in the center. Now notice that, in every direction that dot can move, he approaches the dimension of the Super-Reality in which he is held. There is no up or down for You, Free! Now can you let go?*

ARE YOU LOST? (*PART I*)

You, Free is you, found, in a way.

When you are not free, you are disintegrated, to some extent. In the language of *FoAm*, this takes two forms.

One is the loss of Self in abstraction. An abstraction is a reduction into symbolic form, or conceptual form.

PRIDE PUSHES TOWARD ABSTRACTION, COMPRESSION INTO A LABEL, COMPARTMENTALIZATION AND FRACTURING.

The Self lost in this direction may feel she is 'living in her mind,' is scattered, fragmented, acting a role. In fact, she may feel she inhabits many roles – none of them her whole, authentic Self. Her acedia takes the form of busy-ness, or frenzied activity. She may have reduced her sense of value – substituting money, performance, or appearance as symbols of Self.

She may deal with (dispense with?) other persons by labeling them – substituting this quick sorting for the more difficult process of knowing and being known. She has a filter of preconceptions between Self and Reality, and so her judgements are based on faulty external information.

They also suffer from her lack of connection to internal realities – messages her body and emotions are carrying. She needs grounding in concrete reality, relationship, and rest. She may try to organize and control life (and others?) with words, and to 'explain' reality by building up narratives of experience that justify her actions. There is a thicket of words that must be got through to clear a space where she may encounter reality in true freedom.

Pride – especially pride in self-reliance – pushes you toward this extreme. The great danger of this Loss of Self is this fragmentation into many small, disconnected, unlit triangles

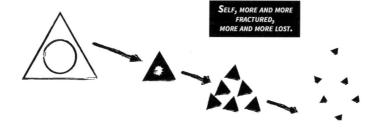

SELF, MORE AND MORE FRACTURED, MORE AND MORE LOST.

This person, tightly pressed, may explode, hurting herself or others, OR she may cave in to the use of drugs, food, alcohol, movies, or porn as a means of at least temporary 'unwinding'.

STOP *Please write about a time when you imploded, got stuck in your brain, or felt fractured. What would You, Today suggest to You, Then?*

ARE YOU LOST? *(PART II)*

The other way You, Free may be lost is, of course, in the opposite form of disintegration:

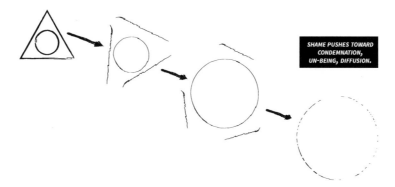

SHAME PUSHES TOWARD CONDEMNATION, UN-BEING, DIFFUSION.

This is Loss of Self by Diffusion. This interior aspect of You, Free, when drawn alone, is a broken or dotted line. This indicates that, like a gas that takes the shape of its container, it has no form outside the boundary of Self. That's the danger of disintegration, dissociation from reality, or un-freedom.

The person trying to find himself without the help of words is gradually 'dispersing' like a gas, into the atmosphere. That atmosphere – peers, culture, nature – may exert some helpful pressure to contain him, but it may also become a substitute for Self. He needs, but resists, clear articulation of Self, moral boundaries, submission to authority, duty, definitions. Instead of opening to feelings, he may be utterly swamped by emotions, with no verbal means of sharing that burden.

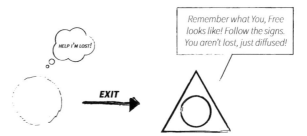

HELP I'M LOST!

EXIT

Remember what You, Free looks like! Follow the signs. You aren't lost, just diffused!

If a peer group becomes a substitute 'boundary' for this Self, it is because he so lacks clear definition and so can act as a mirror for other persons who do not see him in his own wholeness. They love themselves, reflected there.

The diffused Self may begin with a bias for 'just being,' which rightly keeps him from becoming a 'human doing,' but 'laid back' can become 'lazy' and then 'impotent' in the absence of the formal, structural supports integration offers.

Always remember, we are talking about one, whole person in different phases, or aspects of being. Just as pride pushes toward abstraction, shame pushes toward diffusion. They are two sides of the same principle: Negation of the Human Person.

STOP *Please write about a time you've felt ashamed, condemned, lost in another person, or unable to move yourself toward being whole, or being free.*

THE PRACTICE

There is a cyclical nature to the practice of any new skill, but that doesn't mean you are just 'going around in circles,' pointlessly. Look at the phases in the cycle, and you'll see several different skills that need to be learned, strengthened, and integrated.

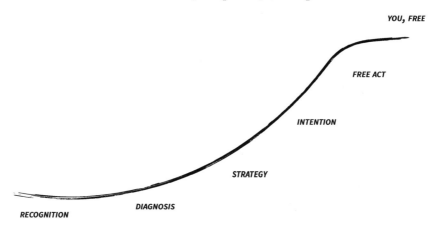

BEGIN the Practice of Freedom the moment you recognize you have lost your freedom. This 'Recognition' or 'Self-Awareness' is the first step.

NEXT, Diagnosis of the state of your own being now that you have become 'caught' in some net, or 'trapped' in some pattern, or 'discombobulated' by some disturbance. Are you stuck in one pole or the other? Are you swinging between them (such as, between rage and despair, or between 'rapidly narrating this story' and 'daydreaming a new story')? Knowing 'where' you are on the spectrum relative to the sweet spot of freedom is critical to getting back.

THIRD, determine what your strategy will be for acting in freedom to respond to the reality you now face. That reality includes you. Your response, to be fully free (and an invitation to freedom, if this involves another person) should not violate yourself, or anyone else. Be careful here! It's really so much easier just to stuff your feelings and move on, no matter the damage that does to your Self. (See 34. Create Your Strategy) Of course, just by beginning the practice, no matter how long you stayed in the prison of un-freedom first, you have begun to execute a helpful and responsive strategy. You are already on your way 'home' at the point when you must decide what to do next!

FOURTH, set your intention. Use your imagination briefly to imagine carrying out the resolution you have chosen, but do not waste much time merely imagining (or you'll be distracted from your true course and tempted either to continue with empty daydreaming, or with imagining the future until that future looks so bleak you collapse in despair).

FIFTH, ACT! Now you're back at the top of the freedom hill. Having just acted in freedom, you now face a new reality. Your act sets something new in motion, and it may very well not be something easy to take. It can be very scary to others, for instance, if you stop engaging in 'polar tug of war' (See 39. Two, Free) and instead invite them to freedom. They may react with a surprise attack. You can't be 'ready' for it, you can only be free. A free act often has immediate and wonderfully transformative effects, too. You may be very pleasantly surprised!

As you continue to enjoy your freedom, your capacity to 'hold on' to that territory increases. At first, though, you may find yourself challenged moment by moment. You will likely miss many opportunities to practice, just because you are over-challenged by all that seems to fight against your freedom. If you are knocked down, it will eventually appeal to you to get up. But if you are on that peak, the practice continues as you resist the push and pull of forces that affect you.

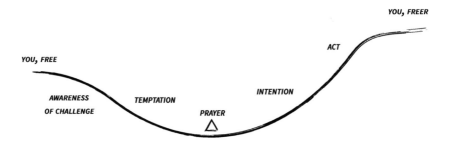

STEP 1 becomes the recognition of a challenge to your freedom, instead of your own state of un-freedom. You've certainly not fallen into bondage just because you feel a challenge to your freedom!

STEP 2 becomes your awareness about how these forces are tempting you to swing over into abstraction or collapse – both, forms of escape from the pressure and both, reactions instead of responses to reality.

STEP 3 is, always and everywhere, the single most important element of your strategy and the decisive turning point in the battle. PRAY for help! Remember: Prayer is PIVOTAL! That triangle is your landmark when you're lost.
    1) The encounter with Reality.
    2) Your awareness of interior tension.
    3) Lift your eyes to the mountain, from Whom help comes.

STEP 4 is now a resolve to act in some way that either deflects or stops or creatively absorbs the force. Just as a fighter learns to turn his opponent's offensive move to his own advantage, you set your intention to respond to reality with the amazing, quantum power of your personal freedom.

STEP 5 is to ACT! Meet the ball with the sweet spot of your 'act racket' or 'bat'. You may hit it out of the park, or fail to connect, but you still have strengthened your freedom. Failure is a great teacher if you carry its lessons back into reflection and strategy creation.

Notice that, in any situation that presents a challenge, if you can recover a sense of your own free agency as soon as possible, you actually feel less challenged. The sense that you are the helpless victim of forces beyond your control is an inner tension that undermines your freedom. Act, in freedom, to repel it. The act may even seem to have nothing to do with the challenge to your freedom.

Perhaps someone you can barely bear to listen to is claiming your time. You feel interior tension because you desire to love and serve them, but are bored out of your mind and have other things to do. Your body feels antsy to get moving, pinned and trapped by this person. The clock is ticking and your other tasks are accumulating. You feel the interior clench of impossible tension and offer a quick prayer asking for the Spirit to help you be present to this person without violating yourself.

In response to the prayed question, "What act in this moment???" you realize you could pick up your knitting, or pare some apples, or do some stretches as you listen. Ahhh…..an act that frees you does not have to be an action against the challenge!

Any free act (the prayer was your first!) opens more interior space for bearing the tension you face, and strengthens the boundary of Self against the 'compressive force,' without violating either of you.

Note also that the overall pattern will always involve some 'dipping' of the curve. The practice of freedom itself demands interior focus away from the challenge and you have permission to back away to recover your freedom. Life cannot be all 'active engagement'. This is one reason the Sabbath is so critically important: it teaches us that we can exercise our freedom by choosing to not act, or to be acted upon. In Sabbath rest, you can find the 'sweet spot' of interior freedom that infuses all your practice with clarity about exactly what state you aim to recover when you move toward You, Free.

The steps of practice each represent a different skill set. You might choose to focus on Recognition for a while, just doing an daily review in the evening to note the moments in which you observed loss of freedom during the day. Take a week for Diagnosis: set a timer and note, several times a day, whether you are feeling 'pointy' or 'circly,' 'unfree,' or 'quite free,' and, perhaps, the circumstances that affected you. If you miss opportunities for practice during the day, note them as practice problems for learning to strategize and create new responses for future use. Granted, you blew it today, but it'll happen again.

The more do-overs, the more practice!

For each of the skills of practice,(Recognition, Diagnosis, Strategy, Intention, Act) write about some situations in which you exercised each one. Choose one to focus on improving tomorrow.

CREATE YOUR STRATEGY

To create a good strategy for reshaping a pattern of un-freedom into a pattern of freedom, you need to understand The Practice and be able to see some of your own experience as a swinging back and forth through freedom into the poles of disintegration. Self-awareness will grow the more you articulate what you learn from the practice of freedom. Journaling is strongly suggested for this journey!

When to design a strategy: *Only* when you are free.

Since, in the beginning, or in difficult circumstances, you may have difficulty holding on to freedom, you may not have much capacity for strategizing. Prayer is not a last resort, but always the first response. Pray. Find your freedom. Then move to Step 1 to create your strategy for the kinds of practice Reality hands you regularly.

STEP 1:

Describe (in writing, or to a friend) the event you face, or the pattern you find yourself repeating, in as much detail as possible.

STEP 2:

Sort out the ◯ and ▲ elements of the Dilemma. See if you and your friend can generate some questions to consider for deeper understanding and more detail.

Example: He comes home. I smell alcohol on his breath. I over-react to his question about what's for dinner.

Over-reaction sounds like jangling: ◯ *What lies am I believing?* ▲ *His question seemed 'pointy'…why? The sense of smell:* ◯ *what associations are triggering my emotions…was this food 'love'? Kitchen = my territory,* △ *it holds and shows my love for family:* ◯ *I exploded… why? What did the explosion accomplish?*

Already we can see some identification of Self with Kitchen, acknowledge that old emotions and associations point to interior knots and old pain, and perceive that some threat of discomfort or violation led to a reduction in freedom and the reactive explosion. Note that this process is not looking for someone to blame, but considering where the free response capacity was lost and the reaction took over.

STEP 3:

Sometimes the whole pattern/event seems to happen all at once. You need to tease out a timeline that helps you discover where a strategy could be most effective. Start with your narrative as written, spread out over a timeline that suggests big spaces lay between the moments as you experienced them. See if you can fill in the spaces with more detail about your actions, thoughts and feelings.

Example:

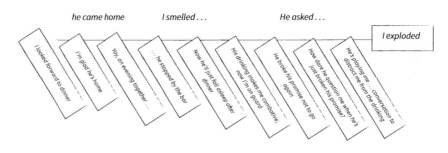

he came home   I smelled . . .   He asked . . .   I exploded

I looked forward to dinner

I'm glad he's home

Yay, an evening together . . .

. . . he stopped by the bar

Now he'll just fall asleep after dinner

His drinking makes me combative;
now I'm on guard

He broke his promise not to go
again

How dare he question me when he's
just broken his promise?

He's playing me . . . conversation to
distract me from the drinking

STEP 4:

Ask questions looking not for blame, but for opportunities to prepare a better plan for free, responsive engagement with this and similar 'realities' you'll face some other time. The more detail you can add to your mental view of this event, the more factors of Reality will be present for you to correspond to.

> *Did you ask for information, or clarification? Did you notice you were experiencing interior interpretations that may, or may not have been correct? Did you make a Good Judgement? Did you construct a quick story to account for the whole situation and justify your reaction? Did you violate your Self – push away your heart's needs, indulge in sin, choose catharsis over freedom? Did you violate the Other – choose not to love, push away a troubling presence, refuse forgiveness, hope for the best? Did you violate yourself, thinking "Just suck it up," or "Don't be a baby"?*

STEP 5:

There are now several points at which you can see that you had a choice to think or act differently. This does not mean you are solely responsible for the event – only that you must find places where your own response-ability was not used to greatest advantage. Resistance to this step indicates you may still be jangling! Don't let yourself be pushed into condemnation, but face this as a new chance to practice freedom. The Accuser doesn't want you to develop a strategy for exiting this pattern!

List every opportunity for a new response that you can see in the scenario you've described. You want to generate a wealth of new possibilities to counter the false thought that there is only one way this scene could play out. A big list should frustrate your slave driver, as it will clearly be impossible to do everything. (See 43. Starting Small) Here are some ideas:

> *I could prepare prayerfully for the possibility he drinks on the way home. He's trying to find freedom, too, and will surely fail a few times. I can help those be 'failing forwards' and not push him into isolation, or condemnation.*

I could focus on keeping my heart open – to love the family with the meal no matter what he does or doesn't do. I could serve it and eat mine in another room if I need some quiet space to support my freedom.

I could rehearse all the reasons I am in love with, grateful to, and happy with my husband so this one slip of his would not overshadow it all.

I can ask God for help letting go of the network of knots - all the other stuff that this jangles - and to heal all the old 'unrequited love' wounds.

I could sing or pray instead of building up steam.

I could label this a 'slip' instead of a 'betrayal' and let him know I'm praying for him to be able to keep his promises to me…be on his side against the destructive behavior instead of seeing him as the enemy…ask him what led to his loss of freedom. Maybe we could strategize together about where he lost his freedom, and how to keep it.

I could see his early bedtime as a chance to do some solitary journaling instead of picturing myself as 'lonely' or 'abandoned'.

I could put on some uplifting music that gets me moving while I finish cooking, to release the tension constructively.

STEP 6:

Choose it. Script it. Write it. Pick just one and determine the best possible wording, whether to speak out to an Other, or to speak to yourself. Eliminate any blame, or snarkiness. Speak the truth in love in self-talk, or in asserting your emotions and needs to another person. (See 44. Seeds & Scaffolds) Prepare to speak as simply as possible, and write it so you can rehearse it if another opportunity for practice looms.

If the pattern occurs a lot, using the same well-chosen words will help the other person (caught in the trap with you) to hear and appropriate your new response. If you act in freedom, your response becomes an invitation to the Other to freedom. A challenge to freedom now triggers a constructive response that can become as habitual as the destructive reactions, with practice.

STEP 7:

As soon as you have an opportunity to use the new strategy, come back to your journal and make notes! What worked? What is still lacking? How can the strategy be tweaked, or more points in the timeline be used next time for a newer-yet response?

Marshal artists describe a slowing down, or expansion of time that occurs as they develop a growing awareness of the many, many small points for action within a battle that looks lightning fast to onlookers. Change your relationship to time to find multiple opportunities for response within these patterns that seem inescapable. (See 42. Free to do Nothing)

Patterns are awful to be trapped in, but their predictability is your ally if you consider each replay an opportunity to practice freedom! God's mercies are new in each situation, and your freedom invites Him to surprise you and your Other by supplying new and gracious responses in place of reactions.

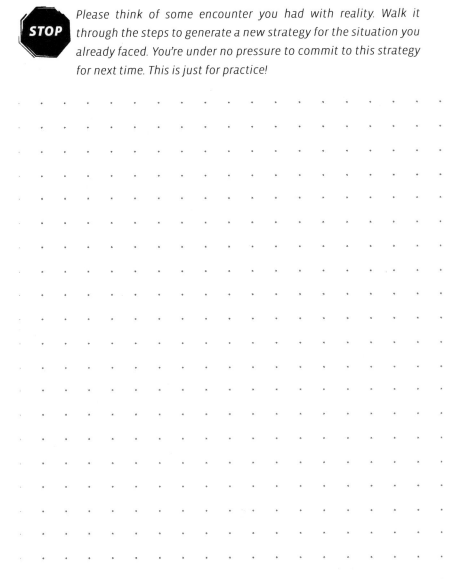

Please think of some encounter you had with reality. Walk it through the steps to generate a new strategy for the situation you already faced. You're under no pressure to commit to this strategy for next time. This is just for practice!

YOUR BODY

Here is your skeleton (rigidity, articulation, form, stable support, limit):

Here are your muscles (fluid movement, action potential, energy, internal strength):

Here is your body moving freely because infrastructure supports organized, integrated action:

(look familiar?)

Here is someone whose bones break under his own weight:

(He's un-free)

This guy has no muscle tone at all:

He's un-free: desire to move doesn't translate into muscle tone, action. You might as well draw him like this:

Perhaps he's been in a body cast and his muscles atrophied. If he doesn't get integrated and get moving, his bones will atrophy, too, without the pull of the muscles.

Hmmm....have you been responding? By every free act, you increase your capacity for freedom! Your responses are cultivating strength, supporting and activating the articulation of Self, generating more and more energy to act.

Respond! Don't skip that step!

This person has physical power to stomp all over others, but no power to be free. You, Free should have an open place to allow others into your own being. Otherwise, you may become a stomper.

THE "MAN OF WILL" IS HUGE COMPARED TO POWERLESS PEOPLE, BUT VERY SMALL COMPARED TO YOU, FREE »

You were made for freedom! Your bones have both structure and lots of open space within. The body is balanced, stable – like a triangle. The pelvic arch directs force down evenly through the feet to secure you on the ground. Arches in your feet give stability and spring to your step. Neck and back curves absorb compression, minimize muscle tension, allow for a full spectrum of movement and movement of interior organs.

The spaciousness of the lungs is made possible by a wealth of infrastructure. Every cell has a cytoskeleton that looks like a geodesic dome opening space through the structural integrity of triangles held in tension. Your DNA is a tiny organizing principle that stamps YOU on every sub-part of your being. It's triangular, like a word, with an opening, growth principle deep inside. You are a living foam of circles in triangles and triangles in circles!

If you feel pain, it may be your body, saying "Come back! Listen!"

STOP *Please, answer these questions: How does your body help you to be You, Free? How is it holding you back? What needs to happen for integration?*

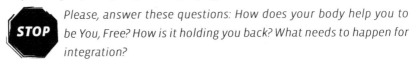

IN THE SWAMP

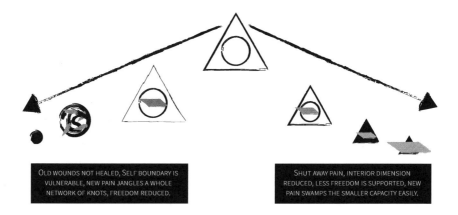

OLD WOUNDS NOT HEALED, SELF BOUNDARY IS VULNERABLE, NEW PAIN JANGLES A WHOLE NETWORK OF KNOTS, FREEDOM REDUCED.

SHUT AWAY PAIN, INTERIOR DIMENSION REDUCED, LESS FREEDOM IS SUPPORTED, NEW PAIN SWAMPS THE SMALLER CAPACITY EASILY.

If you are tied in knots, you may experience 'jangling'. If you shut away all the pain, you may be swamped by it. They are really the same thing. The end result of either dissociation from pain, or of trying not to face pain is the same: You, Un-Free.

Diffused folks often pull themselves back into coherence by believing lies. (See 37. Lies & Violence) They are not 'liars,' but have been easy prey for the Liar who prowls around seeking to unmake disintegrated people. There are, thus, lots of knots tied in them that need untying. That process takes time and may hurt a bit, or a lot. As the song goes, they "haven't got time for the pain," and so various old wounds are held suspended in the knotted matrix of Self.

Next, something new happens and they find themselves way over-reacting. That's a clue that jangling is happening! You snub me at a party and suddenly I am re-experiencing every unresolved rejection of my life. You forget our anniversary and I am swamped by buckets of emotion about all the times you proved you don't really love me. I try to face some deep, unmet needs from my childhood, but then get overwhelmed with sorrow for all the desperately needy children in the world.

Any time something triggers an out-of-proportion emotional reaction, stop as soon as you can to assess what just happened. When your feet are back on solid ground, that's the time to get some words, to articulate what happened, and to set some limits on the imaginations and behaviors that resulted. Create a strategy for the next time (Oh yeah, this will happen again! You need the practice!), and ask others to help you execute that strategy in your hour of need. (See 34. Create Your Strategy)

Panic is an extreme form of jangling, in which one trigger resonates through the whole, knotted network and enormous, non-specific fear swamps you. Perfect Love casts out fear. The most important step in any strategy is to ask for His help and healing.

An interesting trick for getting impossible knots out of a necklace, is to immerse it in soapy water. Remember the image of this gentle, non-forceful treatment. The next time you feel overwhelmed by the generalization of some feeling into a huge compounded 'jangling,' offer yourself a chance to immerse and relax in some safe environment for a while before trying to address the situation. Just knowing that your emotional reaction makes you vulnerable to acting in un-freedom will help you remember to stop and seek freedom before your reaction makes things worse.

A bubble bath, a walk, a friendly cup of tea with a pal, a time of unfocused calm in the sanctuary, or the perfect music can all be ways of relaxing your knots so that it is a free, response-able YOU who decides what to do next.

Abstract folks like to smooth over pain without feeling it. They believe the lie that 'covering' works as an opening principle. It may help them move on in the moment, but at a cost. They may feel superior to people who get emotionally swamped and jangly, but their interior dimension is shrunk by self-protection and avoidance of Self's reality.

Either way that you avoid the need for healing, you reduce your freedom. Why not ask the Great Physician for healing, instead?

STOP *Please jot down a quick list of the various pains you haven't got time for. Be quick. It's not time to face them, just to note them for future reference. When you need 'life material' for your practice of freedom, this is a good list to work from. When the time comes, you'll have help untying those knots.*

LIES & VIOLENCE

This is an organizing principle: △

This is an opening principle: ○

One who is quite closed will feel pressure to find an opening principle. (See 32. Are You Lost? Part 2)

One who is quite diffused will feel pressure to find an organizing principle. (See 31. Are You Lost? Part 1)

A True Principle looks like You, Free: (no surprise!)

The more free you are, the more you will collect yourself around Truth and open yourself to Truth.

An organizing principle that is false is a lie. It looks like this: ▲

An opening principle that is false is a lie. It looks like this:

A lie is a word-without-truth that sucks in light like a black hole. A lie is a truth-without-wholeness that waits to explode, like a bomb. It lacks wholeness because it is self-referential, or truth taken out of the whole context of Truth, or one aspect of Reality that blocks other factors of Reality. Truth, ultimately, must be held in the context of ultimate Being to be fully whole.

If you are quite diffuse, you may clutch at some label that explains yourself, or the situation. You may 'find yourself' in a strong teacher or lover or product. You may submit yourself to the army, or a personal trainer for help strengthening the boundaries of Self through discipline and effort. You may need to do some journaling, or float your thoughts with a friend to articulate clearly a path toward freedom. Watch what happens if you organize yourself around a lie (like "I just cannot change," or "I am not loveable"):

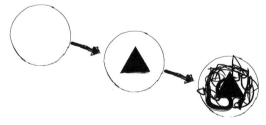

A false organizing principle ties you in knots!

If you are quite fractured, you need an opening principle. Watch what happens if you let a bomb in:

Whew, now you feel better. There's a catharsis that accompanies violence. Problem: You've damaged yourself and probably others, too. Truth is essential for freedom – it is of the essence of the free human person to be ordered to, to correspond to, and to resonate with Truth.

Lies, at either extreme, result in a simple inversion:

You, Tied in Knots is now looking for…an opening principle. The thought, "I shouldn't be expected to bear all this!" may run through his mind. You, Exploded, is now about to close in on Self. Probably the phrase "Shame on you!" will help push him to the opposite extreme of unfreedom. They need healing, grace, true words, interior spaciousness, small steps, an atmosphere of hope, some experience of freedom as a beacon and some path of return.

STOP *Please complete this sentence: "I am powerless to change _____."* *Now, consider whether there are any lies at the root of your impotence. What Truth must you believe to reverse this negation? To believe Truth is a free act.*

FLIGHT & COLLAPSE

Your nervous system responds in two ways to danger. The 'fight or flight' pattern activates your whole being in a tight focus on survival. It looks like this:

If you are utterly trapped or overpowered, the last ditch survival plan is collapse – a death-like shutdown that just might convince a predator to relax his hold, or an opponent to lower his guard. It looks like this:

The trouble is, of course, that you can become locked into one extreme or the other, thus placing yourself in a sort of prison – unfreedom. Victims of trauma may especially need help returning to a free state. Naturally, it looks like this:

The 'jangling' of a practiced, habitual response-to-danger pattern can be triggered by a smell, a tone of voice, a word, a facial expression, or any number of otherwise innocuous stimuli. A narrow focus on a practical goal or outcome can activate a near-constant state of hyper-mobilization, as can the attempt to escape chronic pain.

Ironically, the goal seems to inch further away and the pain gets worse as you lose interior spaciousness. You need an opening principle, not increased vigilance and self-protection. If you fracture, you become a minefield others avoid when you need them most. (See 31. Are You Lost? Part 1)

Overwhelm in the face of foes, fate, or life circumstances – the sense of trapped hopelessness – can activate a near-constant state of hypo-mobilization, dissociative loss of self-boundary, or impotence. Sadly, this person finds no release, but the burden weighs ever heavier as she loses capacity to bear it. She needs structural support. Other people avoid the quicksand of a swamped person, when she needs them most. (See 32. Are You Lost? Part 2)

The integration of Self makes possible both play (mobilization without fear) and intimacy (immobilization without fear). Perfect Love, by the way, casts out fear, which disintegrates you. Note that we keep returning to the need for a person. This is an ultimate and also an immediate need. This need for an Other is actually woven directly into the actual, physical fabric of your being.

The vagus nerve, which modulates your response to perceived danger, touches every major organ. In the absence of perceived safety, it allows the response-to-danger patterns to take over. Your vagus nerve takes its cue from the environment long before your mind, or emotions signal in a way you can consciously perceive.

The 'tone' of this long nerve that runs from base of brain to base of the spine affects every aspect of your being. Positive social engagement does more to 'retune' it to safety and trust and freedom than any other factor.

Movement toward You, Free involves learning to lovingly listen to the body, mind, and emotions. These are subjective truths – factors of Reality that must be understood in order to plot your course toward freedom. Your environment may be priming you for wary self-defensiveness without your conscious choice to be on guard. Low frequency sounds, cues that trigger unresolved trauma experiences, the lack of eye contact or the tone of voice of a person you encounter, and overall lack of well-rested and balanced vagal tone can be factors that compromise your freedom if you are not aware of the possibility. You need help to keep your Self in tune. You are meant to, designed to, co-regulate your state of being with the help of social engagement. If you do not have access to persons, you likely regulate your state with food, alcohol, distractions, and the like. Since you live, move, and have being within a Person, who is always available to you whether you rise up to the heights or go down to the depths, you can learn to have recourse to Him instead. Safety is not absence of danger, but presence of persons!

 Please write about what persons, substances, and activities help you regulate your vagal tone, or social engagement system, or sense of safety.

"FREEDOM IS THE CORRESPONDENCE TO REALITY, IN THE TOTALITY OF ITS FACTORS."

_____

FR. LUIGI GIUSSANI

V. Freedom, Together

Two, Free

You and an Other are sometimes locked into patterns of un-freedom that seem impossible to change. You might accuse the Other of playing 'games' with you, but there is nothing fun about these endless loops. They may push you toward despair if you aren't careful.
Your freedom is a game changer!

As you practice, evaluate and strategize to expand You, Free, you let go of your end of these strange tugs-of-war and generate new responses. By doing so – responding in freedom rather than reacting in bondage to old patterns – you invite the Other to exercise his or her own freedom.

Your response – that does not violate yourself or the Other – is an encounter with a new Reality. He has no pattern to fall back on for a knee-jerk reaction, so may be provoked to a real response.

Consider whether any of your difficult relationships can be described in FoAm terms for some insight into managing these patterns more constructively. Very different people can be held together not in a static 'sameness,' but in a delicate equilibrium of two held in unity by One who loves both. God's Spirit is a golden mean between you, a perfect proportioning movement of Love.

Here are some examples of interpersonal differences that result in tugs-of-war, polarization, demonization of the Other, and similar seemingly impossible-to-resolve patterns. There are many more:

> *Male/Female, Goal-Oriented/Process-Oriented, Adult/Child, Verbal/Visual Thinking Style, Quick Thinker/Deep Thinker, Rich/Poor, Slow Manner/Speedy Style, Employer/Employee, Powerful/ Powerless, Formal/Casual, Conservative/Liberal*

In each pair, one tends toward the 'triangle' and the other toward the 'circle' end of the possibility spectrum. The more free and well-integrated they are as individuals, the better able they will be to integrate with the Other well.

Go back through all the practice lessons to look through this Two, Free lens and see what can be learned. Here's one example:

> *He (△) thinks She (○) wants him to be 'like a woman' when she asks for some behavior that comes naturally to her, but is not easy for him. (Talking about feelings? Picking up socks? Giving gifts? Trusting God? Having fun shopping? Planning trips way in advance?) He resists this pressure by becoming more rigid in his definition of 'manliness,' by toughening his boundary so she can't 'get to him,' by defending his 'role' against the incursion of 'womanly' behavior, or by demanding that she put her emotion-laden requests into concise logical arguments.*

The prospect of becoming more 'circly' may be frightening to him if he perceives those elements of Self as weak, unstable, or exclusively feminine. To her, the prospect of needing to be more 'triangly' in her approach may register as 'more trapped,' 'less happy,' 'too materialistic,' or 'uncared-for'.

Ironically, the more he descends into ▲-ness, the more aversion she will feel for moving toward him. The more she resists verbal clarity, boundaries and 'containment,' or escapes into romantic daydreams and ⌒-ness, the more guarded he becomes against the danger of her position.

Her volatility and insecurity frighten him, so he stands his ground more firmly. His unfeelingness frightens her, so she holds out against being vulnerable to him.

Naturally, they would both do well to find freedom and move toward personal, then interpersonal integration. Meanwhile, even if only one does, it will help. The one seeking freedom is never alone, but has the full support of a heavenly Father, His nurturing Mother, the Church, a cloud of witnesses and, hopefully, some caring friends.

Bring all that support into relationships, and move them toward mutual freedom. Two, Free looks like this: ⟁ You *and* me, without *either* of us being violated. Win-win!

STOP *Please write about some people who provide you challenging opportunities to practice freedom. Can you stop tugging and invite them to be free?*

CONTEXT FOR FREEDOM

Friends help friends be free!

You give me a place in your heart. I see in your eyes that I am beheld – seen truly, wholly – and beloved. I expand in the context of your hospitality.

Conversation is a container where our minds mingle and we voice things we didn't realize until we heard them said to an Other. We both expand in the context of great ideas, shared experience, good advice, and interesting questions.

A womb is a sacred place-of-becoming, where being is held in a rich context with structural interface that mediates nourishment and sensory stimulation. We expand within Mom, Mother Church, the Blessed Mother, and the Domestic Church we call 'home'. We expand within the hearts of those who love us.

Taking our cue from these realities we've all experienced, we can see that a boundaried context can be a space that calls us to expand in freedom. There, a tiny ▲ opens, opens, opens to become more fully realized. The bounded-ness of this context (drawn as an unperforated line) implies that it is held within a larger boundary and so is not a lie pretending to self-containment, which would ultimately violate those within. (See 37. Lies & Violence).

The person you trust, you trust reasonably – not blindly – because they have demonstrable expertise, freedom, defined and limited authority, a common creed, proven virtue. All these are elements that make this a context for freedom. The more a person possesses an infrastructure that is unknotted, aligned to truth, and supportive of his own freedom, the more he becomes a context for the development of freedom in other people.

Our conversation is limited by rules of civility, confidentiality agreements, moral obligation (not to gossip, for example, or to bear false witness), and mutual reverence for objective Truth. It is a context for freedom that can help us to resolve tensions and solve problems creatively. Conversation in the civic sphere is also bounded by laws that govern our society.

A womb is, of course, a context within the boundary of a person, whose freedom, actions, virtues matter very much to its quality. The more mama corresponds to reality, the more this context helps support her baby's growth in freedom.

If you want to be, or to generate, context-for-freedom, first practice being **You, Free**. Grow in definition, limit, boundary, virtue, word power (▲ elements) integrated with growth in affect, receptivity, interior spaciousness and imagination.

Ask yourself, "Can I make space for, make a rich context for, an Other without violating myself or him?" and "How can I imbue this context (me, my home, my office, my conversation, my performance art, my meeting) with hope, safety, nourishment, sensory delight, beauty, light, comfort, blessing, trust, meaning, blessing, value, radiance, and spaciousness?"

To help someone become free, offer him context-for-freedom – in your heart, your home, your music. To ◯, this will be an atmosphere that presses him gently back into coherence. To ▲, this will be a place with enough infrastructure to support his small movements toward expansion and openness. It looks like this:

Context-for-freedom is just enough boundary and just enough radiant openness for the person you invite to be free.

Words that are loving, poetic, combined into interesting stories, spoken gently, or open to personal interpretation are less 'pointy,' while still providing structure for circly folks. Boundaries that have soft edges, more exits, opportunities for personal rearrangement, windows, light, and connection to nature are less 'triangular' and so more inviting to them.

Words that are clearly defined, simple, accurate, spoken with calm authority, less imagistic and emotional, help sharpen up circly vagueness for a pointy person. Clear terms of engagement, respect for time limits, orderly arrangement of elements, and articulation of behavioral expectations (for example: "Gentlemen, please ask the ladies to dance," or "Here, both guys and gals invite each other to dance.") likewise clarify the risky-seeming unknowns of a new and circly situation.

Again, there is no way to please everyone. One man's safety is another's beyond-boredom, and one's warmth and friendliness is the other's too-touchy-feely. To attempt any shape-shifting, people pleasing, or manipulation in order to disarm others is, in itself, potentially risky. The best you can do is to be You, Free, and care truly about the comfort of another in the context you create. Pray for help understanding how best to design context that not only welcomes him as he is, but also invites him higher up, deeper in, and further on toward his own freedom.

STOP *Please list as many different contexts as you can in which you are an actor, and which act upon you. Write about the qualities you perceive in these contexts. Which ones are most expressive of, or supportive of You, Free?*

SEEDS OF FREEDOM

You can create 'seeds' – small forms that open up into great structures. (See 44. Seeds & Scaffolds) You can also become a seed. In fact, You, Free already are a seed. Your ultimate destiny is to be fully realized as YOU within the perfect context of eternity, heaven, and the interior life of the Trinity. The fruits you bear here in the temporal world offer others a taste of this enormous YOU in small bites. The greater your freedom, the greater your capacity to open the eyes of others to the super-reality that frees you.

Fr. Giussani taught that "Freedom is the correspondence to reality in the totality of its factors." To correspond to reality is to be supported by an infrastructure of Truth that links to a greater context of Truth and, thus, forms a ladder or bridge between them. That 'greater context' descends right through Creation to its underlying Logos – the final Word at its origin. It ascends beyond Self toward Self's heavenly destiny in the very heart of God.

Though Reality is seamless, you might picture it to yourself as extending out from you in all directions as three 'orders,' like this:

YOU, FREE AT THE CENTER OF A LADDER WHICH LEADS UP, DOWN, AND OUT TO THE SUPERNATURAL REALITY OF THE ONE WHO HOLDS HIM IN BEING

CREATED/PHYSICAL ORDER

TEMPORAL/SOCIAL ORDER

SUPERNATURAL ORDER

The greater your correspondence to the realities suggested here as three dimensions, or orders of magnitude, the greater your freedom. Without that correspondence, you are, to some extent, a 'knot,' or a disconnected 'node', or a short circuit. God will find alternate pathways, but the thrill of having Him use YOU is one of the great attractions of a life of freedom.
You can't fix everything. You can't wait until you are perfect to offer others a leg up onto your infrastructure, or a word of hope. Ask God's forgiveness for what is lacking in your freedom, and His abundant help to grow in correspondence to Reality. He will pour out grace to others through you, long before you are perfect!

You are a tiny little space God can fill with His sound, His response to the realities you encounter. Freedom is resonance with that sound, or reverberation of that sound through all the interlocking 'tuned strings' in that ladder of proportion. The best you can do is to be You, Free!

To be made quite small so as to permeate hard things and infuse them with light, you need the kind of invisible power that is packed into tiny things like atomic bonds. Stop and think what amazing power is holding the universe in coherence. You can be a tiny vessel for that Love to enter a hardened heart. Your word, your act might continue to affect even a passing stranger for years to come, as it opens within him to reveal some small sound God wants voiced for that particular person.

STOP *Please write about what improvements are needed in your connection to nature, to other people, to God. Consider your knots and disconnections and lack of correspondence. What would it look like for Love to flow freely through your network of connections?*

FREE TO DO NOTHING

A surprising barrier to the development of freedom is your inability to do nothing. Activity can so distract you from the interior awareness of freedom that you miss many opportunities to practice. Busy-ness fractures your time, leaving little-to-none for the pause – the necessary reflective moment for evaluation and strategy creation.

Time, considered as a resource to be used, seems to shrink. Time, ignored as a factor of Reality likewise wafts away like a dissipating gas.

Only when Time is realized to be a rich context for being do you approach freedom – not from Time, but in it.

We don't know Time's ultimate boundary (though we are clear that it has both a beginning and an end), so let's look more closely at its interior dimension – the context of our own becoming. Like any interior, (I draw it with an unperforated line to indicate I am not abstracting it from its 'frame,' or boundary), this context is supplied with an infrastructure, or scaffolding. In the case of Time, you might say the regular, clock-defined hours of the day are its structural elements. They are held within and support a much larger context – surrounded and infused by an opening, expanding principle which turns flat, 2-dimensional clock-time into an enormous, 3-D context for becoming.

The single most important thing you can do to open up this vast space and appropriate it as interior spaciousness is….(drumroll please)…NOTHING.

Nothing! Cultivate the freedom to not-act, to pause, to be acted upon, to relax.

Try this: Exhale, then calmly wait for in-breath to occur. You don't have to force it, or worry that you'll become too empty. It just happens effortlessly when the interior carbon dioxide monitor perceives the time has come.

Try this: Sit down. Now, stand up - watching which muscles you tense, or use. Do it several times to become more aware. Often, the neck and shoulders tense in preparation. Some people rock back, then forward to add momentum to the rise. Others push hands down on knees, or chair, or reach for the support of a table beside the chair. What's your pattern? If you can learn to inhibit the many habitual muscle activations that do not actually contribute to rising from the chair, you may experience a surprising new freedom of this one small movement. Can you rise simply by engaging your leg muscles briefly and thinking 'up and forward'? (This exercise is from the work of Frederick Alexander.)

Try this: Practice Sabbath-keeping your way. On Sunday, offer Time itself into the much greater context of Eternity. Learn to be acted upon, to receive, to open up in correspondence to the Super-Reality in which you live, move, and have being.

When once you experience the freedom of this conscious inhibition of activity, or pause in unreflective forward motion, or interior clearing of the noise and clutter of action, your ability to return to freedom grows. It's a hard 'strength' to describe, because, unlike muscle strength which involves exertion and contraction, it develops by receptivity and expansion. Like muscle strength, though, it responds to practice and becomes more and more amenable to intentional recruitment as it grows.

The experience of freedom in breathing, or movement, or Sabbath-keeping next begins to permeate the other aspects of your whole physical, mental, emotional and spiritual being. It's very much like a tiny open circle of light with the power to permeate darkness.

STOP *Please write about whether your 'tone' is 'too sharp' or 'too flat'. What form of non-action might help 'tune you up'?*

STARTING SMALL

"Do not despise the day of small beginnings." (Zechariah 4:10)

When you believe in free will, it can be very confusing to find you don't often act in full freedom. Remember, "freedom is a conquest." (See 28. Tug-of-War)

You may already be truly free, but it is possible to be un-free to some degree even if you are an adult, secure in your faith, always well-behaved, or quite content with life. Seeking greater freedom is just more of the "growing up in all things unto Christ" that you may already have been doing.

Because 'freedom' refers to an interior state that only you can be sure exists, the practice of freedom must begin with a simple, subjective awareness of Self that may be new even to mature, responsible people. Once you experience that freedom, all of life becomes a playing field of opportunities to practice. The first acts of freedom may be micro-acts: tiny, symbolic, barely noticeable shifts in the core of your being, where freedom originates.

At first, it may be all you can do to grab one opportunity in a day to say "Stop! I will find my freedom before I take one more step." Much of life is lived on auto-pilot, which can be great for setting good habits in the background while 'executive' attention moves to more important tasks in the foreground.

I once asked a friend which ice cream she would choose from the 31-flavors display, and she wasn't sure. She really had no favorite, and usually just took whatever was close, or whatever others were getting. It was fun for her to realize this was an opportunity to discover something (admittedly trivial) about herself and to practice freedom in a teensy way by waiting at the ice cream counter to discover what she actually wanted before ordering. The more important discovery was that she tended to trivialize and push away her own desires…and needs…and feelings. This 'small beginning' was an invitation to more freedom for her.

Please consider that you are not trying to get a Certificate in Freedom, but rather to enjoy as much freedom as possible along the way to an eternal freedom that will dwarf this temporal experience. You are not being judged about your degree of freedom, just invited to the delight of more. Take whatever small step attracts you forward.

STOP *Please write about what attracts you forward and up..*

SEEDS & SCAFFOLDS

You have seen how lies compromise your freedom (See 37. Lies & Violence).

The opposite of a lie is a True Principle – whether an 'organizing' or an 'opening' principle. A True Organizing Principle is a Seed. It looks like this: ⬠ It's so tiny you can barely see the light inside. It is actuality-with-meaning-in-it that, planted, opens up within a person to support his freedom.

A True Opening Principle is a Scaffold. It looks like this: ⬠ It's so tiny you can barely see the window framing the light. It is radiance-with-structure-around-it that, stacked up inside or outside a person supports his freedom.

Words can be both Seed and Scaffold. Acts can be both. Persons can be both. Scaffolding for freedom is largely made of words that a person interiorizes and that then become light-filled structure within him. Seeds of freedom are free acts and words that a person interiorizes and that then become light-filled structure within him. To differentiate them is only to consider how best to approach a disintegrated person. A free person is attracted to light and enjoys climbing ladders. Give him a robust encounter with another free person and they'll both grow.

But a disintegrated person is, to some degree, less able to appropriate light-filled structure. When you design strategies to help yourself during disintegrated moments, or when you want to help someone else, it can be useful to determine whether Seeds and Scaffolds, are needed.

Let's see how this looks in FoAm:

Remember that displaced persons seek the help they need to survive. ▲ needs an opening principle that will not become a destructive explosion. She needs a word that looks like her, that she can trust, that doesn't threaten to open her up too much. She is a smoldering wick and needs an atmosphere filled with oxygen, light, love – a context for becoming that can permeate her defenses and begin to restore her interior spaciousness.

Enter, the Scaffold. This is womb, surrounding and connecting her, making a path for life-to-life transfer. This is an act, a gesture, an embrace with no words, no demands. This is an atmosphere that begins to contain her so she can breathe, can feel whole again, can dare to expand. Beauty has this quality of attractive radiance. It does 'wound' and destabilize a person, but also fills that opening with the presence of a form that supports and corresponds to her need for healing.

◯ needs an organizing principle that will not become a destructive black hole. She needs the meaning, the grace, the love-in-words, but cannot bear feeling their 'pointy-ness'. She is a bruised reed and needs some structural support to gently guide her healing process. Enter, the Seed. This is a true word spoken in gentle love to help her open to the possibility of reclaiming her wholeness and freedom. This is some real thing that gets past her defenses and touches her heart (like the sight of a baby, or a Bach sonata) This is such a little bit of light that she is not threatened with exposure to condemnation. This is a prayer prayed miles away asking Mercy to find a way where there is no way into her heart. This is Christ, harrowing hell, and God becoming small enough to live within her.

So, the word, the fact, the form, the act has both a permeating and a piercing quality. The best ones make a path for the receiver, as he is in this moment, to himself, free - a way where you, or he may currently perceive no way. The best ones correspond to the Love that holds and hopes for the highest fulfillment for the receiver and so, while making no demands, lifts him toward freedom.

Love enables You, Free to correspond to the reality of others by emphasizing the balancing element of your own being, or of the context you create and the words you use. As you learn to treat yourself lovingly, you'll be practicing how to treat others with love. Your practice of freedom is very, very important for the needy, broken world around you!

If someone is un-free, he is dis-integrated, and so his 'circly-ness' will be threatened by your 'triangular features,' and vice versa. You can't be all things to all people, but can appreciate that you may be easier, or harder to approach, depending on the interaction of these factors.

The idea of the 'wounded healer' is common to many faith traditions. A person's ability to see himself as you, like you, is often an important point of contact between you. Unless you can be a bit vulnerable, and allow others 'entrance' at your own weak points, you may find that someone broken just can't quite trust you. Unless you trust God to bring to you those who need your own particularity as a path to Him, you may not develop this freedom to be vulnerable.

 Please think of someone you know who seems 'pointy' and someone who seems 'diffused'. What might you change in your interactions with them, to invite them through You, Free toward their own greater freedom?

THE DOUBLE TWIST

The enemy of your soul has a doubly-twisted strategy for disintegrating and unmaking **You, Free**. Where God wants you to see 'oneness', he tempts you to look at 'many-ness'. And where God wants you to see 'diversity', he whispers "All the same, no distinctions."

When you look inward, trying to understand your own interior dynamics, yearnings, needs and messages, you see a huge inner world, with an amazing variety of objects that mirror everything in the outer world. You have people in your heart, facts in your mind, yearnings in your soul for things that are real (your desire points toward the reality of what you long for). You have a map of the physical, spiritual and emotional spaces you inhabit — lots of information, and different models for processing it all. You find seemingly contradictory elements, and in bearing the tensions that exist between things, you develop strength and resilience. You are *capax omnia* – capable of taking in the whole world. Within you lies a mirror of the universality of God!

But the enemy whispers, "Which is it? Are you a wife, or a mother? A woman, or a whole human being? A chauffeur, or an executive? A happy, or a sad person? A mind, or a heart? Real, or fake? Good, or bad? Worthy, or unworthy?"

He wants your sense of enormity and vast capacity to close in on the false organizing principle that one truth negates another. If he can place realities in a tug-of-war and you can't bear that tension, you might collapse, or let go of one or the other factors of reality in the false belief they can't be reconciled. He wins if you lose your freedom.

But suppose you are feeling the opposite reality, instead. Rather than feeling your greatness, you're feeling your smallness. Then he turns around and does the Double Twist!

Your need for coherence, and for a context of coherence, is fundamental to your integration. When you seek wholeness in Creation that speaks of a Creator, unity among loved ones, or a coherent belief system that helps you understand all of reality, he takes up the opposite lie and tries to scare you with it:

> *"Anarchy reigns out there. There is nothing solid or whole that you can count on. Your family is dysfunctional and disposable. Your God has a thousand faces and you can choose the one you like. Reality isn't even real, you are projecting it all. You can be all things, any number of selves, everywhere at once!"*

He plants the false opening principle that there are no boundaries, hoping you'll lose your grip on the small, concrete, particular, and defined aspects of your being so you get confused and diffuse into nothingness. He wins if you lose your freedom.

When the truth is ONE, INDIVISIBLE, UNITY, WHOLE, SECURE, he plays the 'either/or' card and your interior gaze is clouded by doubt that you are safe, can be healed, can create unities. Conversely, when the truth is UNIVERSAL, ALL, MANY, MULTI-FACETED, CREATIVE, he plays the 'forced oneness' card and spins it the other way.

To split indivisible wholes into fractured parts, or to fuse distinct realities into monstrous amalgamations – either way, is dis-integrating, damaging.

Don't believe lies about Reality. Your freedom depends on correspondence to Reality, and you are a Reality in your own right.

STOP *Please write about a few examples of twisted thinking. Ask yourself, "What things that should be whole are now fractured?" and "What things that should be distinct are now confused?"*

CAPACITY FOR FREEDOM

If you want to increase your capacity for freedom, you'll need lots of support.

External support and internal support should help you move toward your destiny. It is your destiny, dear human person, to correspond so fully to the ultimate Reality that you belong with Him, fit in Him, correspond to, dwell with Him forever!

He is already holding you in His own being. You are much too great and enormous to bear your own Self. You extend over time and He holds the all of you, inviting you into the territory of Self, where you will live forever with Him, in Him.

Let's imagine (Lord, pardon this audacity!) God in terms of FoAm:

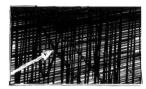

See that? It signifies a Mystery so far beyond my comprehension that my mind reels: God, the untouchable Trinity. If I could make a microscopic triangle with a white so white it would practically flame out of the paper, that would be better.

Here's the interior life of the three Persons of the Trinity:

(Can you see the Love flowing? If we tried to draw that fullness, the circle would seem completely dark. Can you imagine this circle-triangle far larger than all Creation? At least try!)

Now zoom in. Within the roaring ocean of Divine Love, the complete correspondence between the Persons of God generates the matrix of Holy Wisdom.

(If we kept drawing the infinite correspondences, the circle would seem white, empty. Imagine the solid mass of pre-creation, super-substantial Light filling this 'emptiness'. The mind boggles!)

Divine Wisdom, whether shown as a 'black solid' or a 'white solid' would seem to us an impenetrable Mystery, but would indicate both the ▲ of Law and the ◯ of Love fully integrated, waiting receptively for the Person of God to bring it into further expression, further realization, further fulfillment. Into that womb, the Creating Word enters – the Seed unfolding within the Scaffold.

You get the idea: it's triangles all the way down! Our support is a ladder of proportions that is continuous in three dimensions from God to Christ, through Man; from Christ to God, through Creation. Our universe is not floating in an empty void, but contained within a love-filled womb. Man's destiny is to realize that Love and be realized, fulfilled, perfected by Him.

To be free is to correspond to Reality 'all the way up' and 'all the way down'. Your capacity for freedom is increased by an infrastructure of Truth. Your capacity to take in and then to realize Truth is increased by your freedom. All very hard to draw!

Infrastructure supports your capacity for more. Here are two examples:

Lungs: Big, empty bags, right? Wrong.

Structure, filled with structure – capacity made possible by structure.

Interior structure (bronchioles and alveoli), far from taking up room better used for air, actually expands the surface area exposed to air, so that more oxygen can be absorbed. The words you take in, the structures you appropriate, the truth you believe – all build the infrastructure you must have in order to be free. (And to think – God just handed you those glorious lungs for free!)

Bread: Warm, tasty, solid substance, right? Wrong.

Structure (gluten, protein) worked up into a substance whose strands open to enclose fermentation's off-gas. Little pockets of airy emptiness left behind when the gas from yeastie beasties dissipates give bread its texture.

All that work you are doing to practice freedom works up your substance, your 'gluten' into a vessel for grace, light glory.

'Lung' translated into FoAm looks like this:

'Bread' in the FoAm dictionary looks like this:

Any interior held open by infrastructure, like bones, or community, or geographic territory, or ritual ceremony, or music, or a cell, or the interior dimension of You, Free....looks like this:

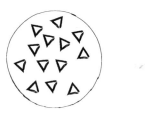

STOP *Please consider what structures hold open your freedom, and how they multiply to expand it. Just thank God for whatever is serving you in this way right now.*

But My Situation

Your situation is different. I know. Why do I think I can speak of your freedom when I don't know your details?

Here's why: Because freedom is *of the essence* of human being. I don't have to guess whether you're one of those called to freedom. I know it.

All those particulars of your situation and circumstances? Accidents. Every single aspect of your particular life is an opportunity to practice freedom. You, Free is an eternal being destined to move freely within the triune Being of God; freely between the New Heavens and New Earth; freely among angels and eternal human beings; and freely in the territory of your own Self.

But there's one catch: As Fr. Giussani says, "the solution doesn't lie in the plane with the problem." You've got to look up. The problem with problems is that the focus on 'solving the problem' keeps your gaze horizontal. You aren't fully free to respond until your gaze moves vertical

The fullest possible freedom is only possible for you with God's help. You cannot accomplish the full integration, healing, wholeness, or freedom of yourself any more than you can raise yourself from the dead, or generate your own child. At every point, then, where you are challenged to find your freedom, the best first move is to ask God for help. It's Good Judgement to respond to every situation with this Primary Strategy: PRAY!

The practice of freedom reminds you to then act in accordance with the Good Judgement God helps you to form in response to the Reality you face. St. Teresa of Avila saw prayer itself as a three-part process:

> 1. *Understand the spiritual reading, or sermon* △
> 2. *Be Affected – What is your heart's response?* ○
> 3. *Resolution – What act will carry forward this moment with God as word, act, substance into the world?* △

You are God's response to the particular realities only you encounter. Prayer like this prepares you to resolve tension creatively.

Since freedom is "correspondence to reality," you can grow in every encounter with reality. In that encounter, something's got to change, shift, be made new. You! You might be able to change the particulars of the reality you face, but the shift first needs to occur in you. Reality doesn't change, but your relationship to reality really changes the whole situation.

Think of reality as a pointy, actual, weighty, prickly 'something' external to your Self.

It affects you. Let's say it causes discomfort, pain, or tension (because pleasant realities are easy to deal with…just beware of lies in circular or triangular clothing). To correspond to it is, first, to respond. As you take it in and respond to the tension or discomfort, you appropriate its structure to some degree.

Ouch! Reality hurts!

You can try self-defensive tightening of your boundary. You can try closing up your interior dimension to guard it. You can collapse and be overtaken to release the tension. You can run and hide, but you'll carry the Thing with you because it has affected you. Only by responding do you make that intrusive reality a building block of Self.

The memory of a trauma can continue to trigger the original terror, or grief. Whatever frightened you continues to play upon your emotions long after the real Thing is gone. The pain you are trying to block out with distractions becomes a weight you drag around constantly. When reality affects you, you can't pretend away that new interior imprint of the encounter.

Growth in the capacity to bear and resolve tension is growth in freedom, interior spaciousness, maturity, correspondence to Reality. Here are the three steps to freedom:

1. ENCOUNTER REALITY

What is the Reality you face? What Form is mediating that Reality to you? Be present to what is real here, and discount what is imagined. Look through the surface to see more fully. Articulate, but do not hide behind labels and false narratives.

2. BE AFFECTED

You will be tempted to just take it in, or walk away, ignore the Affect, and get on with your life.

What attracts you? What provokes you? What tensions are present in the situation, in yourself? What is your heart, your gut telling you? Articulate the affect, but do not avoid it by blaming, or intellectualizing.

3. RESPOND CREATIVELY

The internal and external reality, the self and other, the competing goods, the struggle await your judgement. Once you articulate your intention, seek some act by which to realize it. True creativity requires the help of the Spirit.

Pray for His action upon the tensed string within you. Once you know what to do, do it: act, speak, create form. The best act may be to not-act, to STOP longer to recover your full freedom, to rest a bit from the struggle.

Your response may need to be very tiny for you to accomplish it!

Creative Resolution generates new form, invites others to freedom, changes the next bit of Reality you face, and violates neither you nor the Other. The new 'form' you create may be an act, a gesture, or an actual form such as a painting or a batch of cookies.

Practice whenever you are learning something new, interacting with human beings, praying, growing in virtue, out in nature, at Mass, giving or being offered a gift. You won't be able to practice constantly. You may have one, or twelve, or fifty moments of conscious, free, responsiveness to the realities that intersect your path.

The more free you become, the more attraction the opportunities have for you. Truly, he who has will be given more. The rich get richer, and this is why.

Please write about the particulars of your situation. If you had been keenly aware of them all day today, how many opportunities might you have chosen from for practicing freedom? These are your 'life materials,' and your practice of freedom is turning your life into a work of art!

OBSTACLES

When you aren't free, obstacles seem huge, impenetrable, impassable.

The obstacle you face may be a wall, a limit, a to-do list, a bad knee, an overdrawn bank account, a plate of cookies, an enemy – anything that seems like a barrier between you and **You, Free**.

It may seem to block you, swallow you up, overshadow you. It will still be there once you are free, but it will seem smaller. It won't change, but you will.

Or, you may find yourself in a hostile context. A disintegrating context may be full of lies, full of empty chatter, full of awful noise, full of filth or clutter – anything that seems to crush you instead of supporting your growth in freedom. It really is just an obstacle that surrounds you.

Either way, you feel small, and IT looms large. You need something larger to focus on. The solution doesn't lie in the same plane with the problem.

There's a light shining that is bigger than you, bigger than this obstacle. Somewhere, down the path that leads through this obstacle, past this moment, is a place where you are growing free. Lift your eyes to that mountain. An Integrating Context exists that dwarfs this obstacle, and an Organizing Principle waits within you to dispel this darkness.

Within the One who is greater, you find a spaciousness that allows you to rise above the barrier, and move toward You, Free.

Even in darkness, light radiates from the One who became small enough to enter your smallness. You, Free is just a prayer away!

 Please, will you list the obstacles you face to becoming free?

FREEDOM IN TIGHT PLACES

Full freedom is impossible. It is a supernatural state that can only be approximated by the kinds of freedom you can experience in your own strength. Your best opportunities to practice are, therefore, impossible situations. When you reach the point at which you actually cannot, you are at the threshold of the glorious freedom of the children of God. There, you can do all things through Christ, who strengthens you.

'Impossible' happens even when you aren't looking for an excuse to give up. There's an abyss of impotence (See 28. Tug-of-War), where your rebellion may dump you. You may avoid facing your weakness just because you wrongly believe it is such an abyss. But weak-and-seeking-help is a very different thing from choosing-weakness-over-freedom. When you must and would-but-cannot, a different possibility opens: ask for God's help.

Here are a few examples:

Joni Erickson Tada, quadriplegic for over 30 years and a vibrant witness for the power of Christ to give her an abundant life, still sometimes thinks, "I can't do quadriplegic today," as she faces the daily ordeal of being dressed and fed by attendants. In those moments – utterly bereft of strength to face an unshakeable reality that seems to prevail over her freedom – she offers Christ her weakness, her emptiness, her 'cannot'. Her life's testimony is the transformation of all the 'impossibles' into the glorious freedom and joy she shares at every opportunity. You'll have times when you "can't do quadriplegic today," and they will help build your freedom.

St. Maximillian Kolbe – concentration camp prisoner – made one of history's most memorable acts of full freedom when he offered his life to save another prisoner. No guard, no inmate, no hearer of this story and – most important – none of those he accompanied to death through slow starvation in a sun-baked, windowless bunker were left in any doubt that his unquenchable strength was the power of Christ within him. His free act was an invitation to freedom for every human being it touched. There will be moments when you can freely offer what nobody can rightly demand of you, and they will help build your freedom.

A mom at home with children experiences many moments when she must – carry the unborn child, change the awful diaper, tend to the midnight vomit, nurse through excruciating pain. She may develop heroic strength of her own, but certainly will face some impossible tensions between her needs, strengths and desires, and those of her loved ones.

Full freedom is the rare and precious fruit of Practice like this. The highest freedom is to do what you must, freely. Most such acts go unnoticed, so it is critically important that you realize their 'results' are to be found in your own Self. One of the great gifts of 'impossibles' like these is the growth of your detachment from end results. Demand for results, or attachment to expectations for particular outcomes is one of the hardest-to-eradicate impediments to your interior freedom. Thank God if you are called to tiny, hidden, numberless acts of freedom, as there is no better practice for You, Free!

Whatever impossible reality you face, you might be tempted at first to butt heads with it in your own strength. We call this 'trying hard,' and it is dangerous.

Trying Hard looks like this:

See those muscles tightening, that mind focusing on The Problem, that brow furrowing, that belly bracing with readiness? What's happening to the interior dimension? It's growing smaller. Just when you needed greater capacity to bear Reality, your Trying Hard reduced you. There may be some pride involved in Trying Hard. After all, how will anyone know how nobly long-suffering you are, or how sorry they should feel for you if you don't seem to be working hard, sweating, suffering, *doing*?

Here's another common reaction to an impossible situation. Closing the Case looks like this:

In a misguided effort to deal with reality before you actually encounter it, you fill that space with vain (impotent, pointless) imaginations. You place imaginary barriers up and Reality comes along anyway, but now you are full of false supports instead of spacious to meet it! No wonder you collapse under the weight of your own self defense strategy and end up in the Abyss of Can't! Here's how you look when you stave off encounter with reality this way:

You have very little actual, real, spacious, interior freedom with which to meet reality when you try to close the gap between you and It imaginatively. Think of vain imaginings as a sort of miasma over the Abyss of Can't. Flight into unreality drags you down into that abyss. Your 'case for the defense' has made you more likely to despair, and then to sin in your despair. Add to the exterior 'compressive forces' the new interior tension of having betrayed yourself. (Memo to self: despair always leads to sin!)

What huge 'factor of reality' have you failed to take into consideration? The Presence of God! Your mind went from 'impossible' to despair rather than to the Source of the help you needed. If reality is coming, pray for help to meet it. If you notice a Vain Imagination (reward being given to you for your action, knight in shining armor, winning the lottery, family suddenly working as a team to help you, Self as tragic hero in impending drama), cast it down! Pray for a mind clear of misleading images with which to open to reality and respond to it creatively.

If you hear the words "case closed," that's your despair masquerading as your defense attorney! No reality is closed, or impermeable to God's grace. NO CASE IS CLOSED to the Just Judge!

Your Vain Imaginings might take you off into the future. Depending on the narrative you write, the current reality could seem to disappear effortlessly, or the current demand could grow to monstrous proportions until – even if you did face it today, you'd finally collapse anyway, so you might as well give up now. Whether you're imagining the worst or the best, you can't find the grace you need to *actually* act, now, in response to reality. There is no grace in an imagined future.

◯ is resisting being 'pinned down' into the present moment, but that's where Christ meets and responds to reality from within You, Free.

Childlike ◯ may also be feeling that the need for hard work is 'punishment,' and thus be pushed toward collapse by shame. Putting words to that dynamic helps hold her interior freedom 'open' even during a difficult struggle (See 44. Seeds & Scaffolds). 'Circly-ness' in the face of impossible tension may also be a mask over, or reaction to, a knot of interior demand. Full freedom makes no demands for outcomes, but it is completely natural to have hopes and desires and expectations. To have them is one thing, but to demand them is to attach to them as false organizing principles.

For example, I can try a new strategy with my husband in the hope that he responds in a certain (and reasonable-to-expect) way. I lose my freedom when I act *with an interior demand for* that outcome.

I realize that I didn't act in full freedom when feel myself tied in knots about the non-outcome, or react explosively to that next reality.

An act only becomes an invitation to the freedom of the other person when it is *actually* free.

 Instead of toughness and props, you may try to diffuse the tension with alcohol and other escapes. Now you look like this:

Once your Self breaks down, you might collect yourself around the lie that 'impossible' means 'not possible,' when really it just means 'not possible without God's help'.

Just remember, true freedom lies not in your imagination, or in your self-defense, but in your invitation to God to make His strength perfect in your weakness.

Vain Imaginings

You, Free: Open to the action of God, filled with His supportive grace and His Word, held safely in His Presence, able to respond creatively

Self-Defense

STOP Please note any 'vain imaginings,' self-defenses, props and escapes that may be interfering with God's desire to do the impossible.

CORRUPTIONS OF FREEDOM

Freedom can be described as a via media between the corruptions of ▲ legalism and ○ license.

Legalism values means as ends in themselves – laws, forms, words, institutions meant to be structural supports for freedom of the human person are, removed from the context of that meaning, flat and 'window-less'. License rejects means as necessary, thus valuing a formless *ideal* of freedom without reference to the *actuality* by which persons come into possession of freedom, or appropriate the necessary infrastructure for freedom.

These corruptions may be accompanied by distortion in your understanding of the nature of Truth. In a reactive defense against the modern notion that truth is relative, you may tighten up your triangle of Objective Truth to such an extent that Truth is reduced, flattened, or abstracted from Reality. Only when the human person is restored to the idea of truth does it become whole. The person, or subject, is a factor of Reality – the tension he feels, the struggle he faces, the response he makes.

Subjective Truth is rather like Truth's 'interior dimension'- subordinate and complementary and necessary to the fullness of Truth. Taken as an opening principle, unboundaried Subjective Truth begins as an 'atmosphere of freedom' and ends as a vacuum that kills freedom.
Taken as an organizing principle, unequivocal, objective truth begins as a strong foundation for freedom, but ends as a strong man who usurps freedom.

These corruptions of freedom and truth are formational, pushing persons toward polarized personhood, away from freedom.

You, Free are the means God has chosen for the realization of Christ, His very Image. Legalists may have forgotten the importance of your integrated wholeness, interior spaciousness and voice. The licentious have surely forgotten your need for boundary, true doctrine, practiced virtue and concrete means of grace. It's up to You, Free to aim for the whole Truth that actually sets you free. He looks like this:

And You, Free are meant to look just like Him!

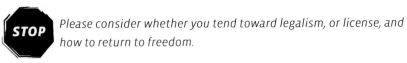

STOP *Please consider whether you tend toward legalism, or license, and how to return to freedom.*

FoAm, My Love Language

Here's the story behind my use of the triangle-circle 'language' I call FoAm, for *Fons Amicus* – Fountain of Love.

It all started when I was asked to speak to the Collaborators of the Apostles of the Interior Life about the beginning of the interior life. I prayed about how to discuss the early stages of spiritual life with people who probably had already matured quite a bit spiritually. Where there is a paradox, I look to the Spirit for a creative resolution.

I was inspired to try to recover a sense of childlike simplicity through the use of construction paper symbols and a visual metaphor for interiority. The talk really seemed to click, but the big surprise didn't hit me until much later.

In the weeks and months following that talk, I found myself, as usual, in a lot of conversations with friends that involved our trials and troubles. Over and over again, I recalled that 'triangle talk' and used that metaphoric/symbolic approach to illustrate all my wise advice. Concepts I used to find hard to get across were now sailing into friends' consciousness to the extent that we began to use the triangle-circle as shorthand for all kinds of related ideas.

It seemed I had hit upon an 'elegant solution'. Matthew May's *Pursuit of Elegance* explains beautifully what elegance means:

> "*…what sets [an elegant solution] apart is the unique combination of surprising power and uncommon simplicity, and that elegance entails achieving far more with much less when faced with a complex problem.*"

May tells us that elegance is characterized by four qualities: Symmetry, Seduction, Subtraction, and Sustainability. Symmetry involves repeating patterns, beauty and balance. "Seduction addresses the problem of creative engagement. It captivates attention and activates imagination…Leaving something to the imagination, open to interpretation…" Subtraction is about doing more with less, conserving, adding value by taking away. Sustainability "implies a process that is both repeatable and lasting".

So, I think the Holy Spirit actually gave us an elegant language in which to speak of things human and divine. The symbols help generate metaphors by which two things – such as objectivity and subjectivity, or law and love can be held in relationship as an integrated unity that may be explored and experienced. Words themselves have always done this very thing. The addition of visual symbols speaks to a time in which, for many people, words seem foreign, complex, forbidding, or otherwise inaccessible.

From a linguist's perspective, a language is a 'real language' only if it has the capacity to generate new concepts and communicate them. Because FoAm does this, I confidently call it a language. Wives have taught their husbands to speak it, my kids find it easy to understand, and it keeps generating new concepts. It's an elegant, visual symbol system that helps us articulate and consider relationship dynamics and more.

Since FoAm is derivative of and dependent upon the English language, my task has been to clothe its visuals in just enough verbal structure to give them to others. FoAm itself depends upon an integration of its 'circle' and 'triangle' elements which is vastly easier in person than on paper!

I have found that this conversation, is very accessible even for people who are still quite guarded, or who don't usually reflect on and discuss the dynamics of their inner workings, or relationships. It seems to give them a tool, a vocabulary, for discussing the reality of their own disintegration, bondage, balance, etc.…

It gives both metaphoric access to, and verbal distance from deep and difficult, or dynamic and difficult realities. FoAm, supplied with the user's own 'life materials,' becomes within him alive with meaning.

FoAm is a way of helping you draw on your own wisdom about what you need, what to ask for in prayer, how to respond to the realities only you face. No answers to problems are supplied, because they need to be voiced by you. Every book is a conversation in its way, but this one is nothing without that conversation.

I typically scratch out diagrams wherever I find myself in these conversations, spontaneously and informally. I've drawn them in beach sand, on frosted windows, on cocktail napkins, and in book margins too many to count. Since I speak with my hands, anyone who knows me also knows how to place their hands into the perfect, integrated circle-triangle when discussions lead – as they so often do – right back to a via media and thus, to FoAm.

Artists will groan at the graphic immaturity of the visuals, but Everyman will be able to reproduce them effortlessly.

Ironically, 'pointy' people are likely to look at FoAm and say how simplistic and silly it looks, while 'circly' people may look and see just 'too many words'. You can't win 'em all!

We who 'speak FoAm' might consider ourselves, then, a small 'community of practice.' As the 'hub' of what I hope will be a growing number of people in that community, I would love to serve as a collection-point for your feedback, questions, and further insights about You, Free. If it is a gift from the Fountain of Love, it is given to us, not to me. Please, please let me know what you think, what you experience, what more you need. You can easily contact me (respond please!) at CharlotteOstermann.com, charoster@outlook.com, or Director@JoyFound.com.

Your response will make my day! Thank you for reading and being You, Free.

Examples From Practice

Members of the FoAm 'community of practice' have kindly allowed me to include some of their thoughts and experiences and journal entries:

> *"It would not be an exaggeration to say that the circle-triangle idea has helped me to understand reality—what is. I have been able to use it as a hermeneutic for life! Through it, I better understand what God desires for my life, what Christian freedom is, and what it means to be like Christ, the free and perfect man."*

> *"Letters I wrote in my journal:*
> *Dear Pointy Me, You scare me! I'm afraid you'll demand more of me than I can give…that you only value getting stuff accomplished…that you'll run off and abandon me. You get impatient and shift to a new game plan that would work if only I weren't there like a wrench in the gears.*
> *Dear Round Me, Well, sorry, but I am impatient with you! You just drag and drag against the possibilities I want to see realized. I'm trying to have courage here, to act, and you collapse right when I need to be able to count on you. At some level I just don't trust you. I'm fighting integration because I feel it will result in my disappearance.*
> *Dear Pointy, Me too! I'm afraid I'll be destroyed.*
> *Dear God, where is the path out of this awful self-betrayal. How can we/I be safe here?*
> *Dear Round Me, Maybe you need to trust more that it really is God who is calling us, and I need to trust more that Christ is present within to protect us."*

> *"For decades, I struggled with crippling anxiety which robbed me of happiness and prevented me from doing many normal, everyday things. The circle-triangle language gave me the understanding of the freedom to which God has called me: to inhabit and expand my interior spaciousness in situations that made me feel constricted and afraid, and to assert the boundary of my being, that I should never violate myself in an attempt to overcome my anxiety. By choosing tiny acts of freedom in difficult, anxiety-provoking situations—truly only offering what I could offer in freedom—I was gradually released from many of my gripping fears. I learned to employ physical techniques to*

bring myself back into balance. I can truly say that You, Free has helped me to embrace God's call to freedom."

"I had been deeply wounded by a family member, which was causing great anxiety and anger in my life. When the ideas of You, Free were introduced to me, I was set down a path of healing. First, I learned to create healthy boundaries in my relationship with this person. In all of our interactions, I was guided by the knowledge that my own growth in interior freedom could call him to greater freedom and that we could, through God's grace, grow toward wholeness and a rehabilitated relationship. Then I started to offer only what I could offer in freedom: I prayed for the desire to forgive him and to want to want to pray for him. Over time, God gave me the capacity for these things. I can now say that this relationship is largely healed and that I have been brought to a place of wholeness and freedom in my being."

"The counsel of a friend using FoAm helped me see that just one person in a relationship can make a big difference. Being response-able doesn't mean I'm to blame for everything. Being free doesn't mean everything changes, but I can sure affirm it changes everything!"

"Here's a sort of poem I wrote 'to' someone who seemed to be rejecting everything I offered. The triangle-circle helped me see this impossible situation very differently:
My heart was full of love for you. I offered it freely and you rejected it. You prefer the dark, cramped space of life without me to the possibility of being you, being free, being whole, being one with me. Where does that leave me? Love offers you enormity, but you are small; offers you greatness, but you are narrow; offers you gift, but you are too stingy to receive; offers you freedom, but you prefer the prison you have built. I want to be free. I want to be like Love, wounded. So…I'll return again and again to be offered, and to invite you to freedom."

"FoAm helped me with time management. I couldn't figure out why sometimes my systems worked and other times I resisted them. Now I see how I can lay out plans to take my circly-ness and triangle-ness into account better. I've been working with the circle-triangle language in my journal to get more integrated and reduce my self-defeating, self-undermining patterns."

"FoAm changed my relationship to food! I finally understood I was eating to stabilize the swinging pendulum and now I'm free of that."

"Thank you for helping with the dynamics of my marriage. I understand my husband so differently now, and have real hope we can grow better integrated even if he doesn't do much to help."

"I was being bullied and watched as you put words together to help stop the bullying without violating that person. It really helped to see you start from the circle-triangle analysis, then build a 'verbal structure' as you call it, to invite them to freedom. They still do it, but mama's got a whole new game plan! Thanks much."

Souls at Rest, in FoAm

AN EXPLORATION OF THE EUCHARISTIC SABBATH

Souls at Rest – An Exploration of the Eucharistic Sabbath could have been written in FoAm. I offer an approach to Sabbath-keeping that corresponds to your freedom.

Instead of a collection of prescribed
and proscribed activities,

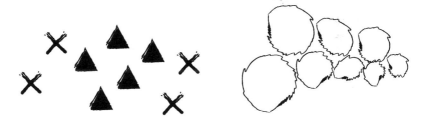

or a program of diffused inactivity,

I suggest that the Sabbath be approached as a 'tonic'. It restores you to freedom from either mode of disintegration.

As the highest, smallest, most powerful Presence of Christ, the Eucharist lacks nothing. We, however, lack much in our capacity to appropriate its gifts. The Sabbath offers a contextual matrix of support for the development of greater capacity.

The Eucharist is held like a seed within the scaffold of the liturgy – a richly appointed context for its unfolding, or communication. The Mass is held like a radiant jewel within the Sabbath day that can become, with your practice of freedom, a wide-open receptivity to the Lord of the Sabbath.

A Sacrament, and particularly this Sacrament, is Substance with Eternity in it, Law with Love in it, symbol filled with the very substance of that which it signifies, or in FoAm: △

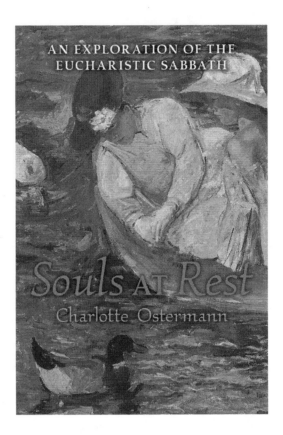

"I KNOW OF NO BETTER TREATMENT OF THE SUBJECT . . . CHARLOTTE HAS GIVEN A GIFT TO US IN REVEALING THE WISDOM OF GOD'S CALL TO REST."

DAN BURKE, AUTHOR OF *NAVIGATING THE INTERIOR LIFE*

ORDER *SOULS AT REST* (PUBLISHED BY ANGELICO PRESS) FROM AMAZON.COM OR THROUGH YOUR BOOKSTORE.

Souls at Work, in FoAm

AN INVITATION TO FREEDOM

Souls at Work – An Invitation to Freedom is undergirded by my experience using FoAm as a help in the practice of freedom. I define freedom as the ability "to wield myself according to my own desires, and to yield myself according to God's desires."

To surrender to God without fear is to open to intimacy.

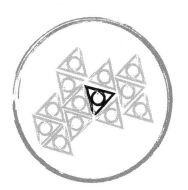

CHRIST, THE FREE MAN, RE-ESTABLISHES YOUR RELATIONSHIP TO REALITY, REALIGNS YOU TO GOD, RESTORES YOUR FREEDOM.

To wield the Self is to take the territory of Self. God's own Word stands within You, Free is the new and sovereign Organizing Principle. This territory is not your own, but is claimed in His name. To expand the territory of Self and to dwell in it richly, is to be free.

Souls at Work offers practice in bearing tension, in formation of the infrastructure of Self through metaphor, in engagement with the sometimes-hostile wider culture, and in creative resolution of the great paradox that your work is to become you, fully realized, through cooperation with the grace of God.

Souls At Work

AN INVITATION
TO FREEDOM

Charlotte Ostermann

"…SELF-HELP BOOKS ARE A DIME A DOZEN, BUT CHARLOTTE
OSTERMANN REINVENTS THE GENRE, GIVING US A BOOK TO LIVE
WITH, TO DREAM WITH, TO WORK WITH. IF YOU ARE A TEACHER, OR
A HOMESCHOOLER, OR IF YOU SIMPLY WANT TO BE 'FULLY HUMAN,
TRULY FREE,' YOU WILL FIND WHAT YOUR SOUL NEEDS IN CHARLOTTE'S
GENTLE WISDOM."

STRATFORD CALDECOTT, AUTHOR OF *BEAUTY FOR TRUTH'S SAKE*

ORDER *SOULS AT WORK* (PUBLISHED BY ANGELICO PRESS) FROM AMAZON.COM OR THROUGH YOUR BOOKSTORE.

Topical Cross-Reference

Other Books by Charlotte Ostermann

"THEREIN LIES THE NOBILITY OF THE FAITH:
THAT WE HAVE THE HEART TO DARE SOMETHING"

BL. CARDINAL JOHN HENRY NEWMAN

Ostermann takes up Cardinal Newman's challenge,
giving readers the heart they need to live faith as a daring
adventure.

Essays accompany each poem to make it more accessible,
allowing readers to understand allusions, invented words,
spiritual ideas, and the craft of poesis as they learn with the
poet to read, hear and pray with poetry.

The person of the poet emerges from the interplay
between essays and poems, as a spiritual mentor and
companion in faith. *A Destiny to Burn* invites readers to
experience themselves as masterpieces – *poiema* – crafted by
the hand of God.

About the Author

Charlotte has been weaving poetry and faith together for many years as a spiritual mentor, author, and inspirational speaker. She is the author of *Souls at Rest – An Exploration of the Eucharistic Sabbath, Souls at Work – An Invitation to Freedom, Souls at Play – Reflections on Creativity and Faith* (in progress), *Making Sunday Special, Life in Motion, Dare Your Something,* and *Elizabeth of the Epiphany. A Destiny to Burn* is a collection of her published and unpublished poems, with reflections and reading notes. Some have served as the core of her talks and retreats.

Charlotte's poetry workshop, *Playing with Words*, has been custom tailored for retreats and workshops, and schools. Her poems, book reviews and articles have appeared in Canticle, St. Austin Review, Gilbert, Thessauri Ecclesiae, the Cardinal Newman Society Journal, and elsewhere. She is a blog-contributor to Catholic Exchange, Catholic 365, Roman Catholic Spiritual Direction, and Catholic Writers Guild.

Charlotte is a founding member of the Family of the Apostles of the Interior Life, the Living Poem Society, the Catholic Creatives Salon, Sursum Corda Polyphony Ensemble, and the Northeast Kansas Chesterton Society. She blogs, consults with non-profit organizations, speaks about holy leisure, education, poetry, rhetoric, creativity and cultural redemption, and directs the Joy Foundation – a small non-profit dedicated to Catholic cultural initiatives (JoyFound.org). Please visit CharlotteOstermann.com for more information and an easy contact form.

About the Designer

Cameron DuPratte is an artist and designer fron Lawrence, Kansas. A graduate from The University of Kansas in Visual Art, he now handles a wide variety of projects, from educational materials to music promotion, on top of a mountain of personal work–all of which can be seen on his website, www.camerondupratte.com.

When he is not working on his computer or covered in paint, you may find DuPratte and his wife feeding their many reptiles or playing Dungeons and Dragons with their friends.

MotherheartPress

Motherheart Press is a project of the Joy Foundation. Motherheart resources support Catholic families, Catholic artists, Catholic educators, and those who build Catholic culture in other ways. All proceeds from the sale of Motherheart books support Joy's various Catholic cultural initiatives.

Contributions to Joy are also gratefully accepted, and support such projects as Catholic book study groups, 50 Million Names, Sursum Corda Polyphony Ensemble, Most Pure Heart of Mary Catholic Youth Choir, Catholic Creatives Salon, Northeast Kansas Chesterton Society, Poetry workshops for Catholic schools, Chesterton Society's Digital Chesterton project, grants to Catholic artists and iconographers, Joyful Moms Workshops, Regency Guild dances, Jubilate Deo children's choir, a resource lending library and Bright City. Joy also sponsors Charlotte's speaking engagements for groups that can't afford speaker fees.

Several Motherheart books are available for free download at MotherheartPress.com. Charlotte Ostermann, Joy's Director, welcomes you to receive, participate, donate, and respond…FREELY! We ask that you do not photocopy or scan, but refer others to MotherheartPress.com. Your referral is more support for Joy.

You're invited to watch a brief video about the Joy Foundation at www.JoyFound.org.

FoAm—What's Next?

Look for more FoAm & Freedom on my blog at CharlotteOstermann.com.
Coming soon: the next two volumes in the 'Freedom Trilogy' – *Full Spectrum Freedom* and *3D Freedom.*

New Elegant Lessons in Freedom include:
- Reflection & Translation
- Trigonometry & Time
- Fractals-in, Fractals-out
- Mother & Father Wounds
- The Excellent Reader
- Sensing the Sweet Spot
- Sound & Story
- Figure-Ground Shift
- Freedom & Habitude
- Form & Freedom
- Context & Content
- Reciprocity, the Lost Art
- Cancer & Heart Failure
- Tense & Tension
- Dynamic Equilibrium
- Ratio & Proportion
- Turbulence & the Well
- The Work of the Middle

Your feedback can only enrich this work. Please let me hear from you!

" The most real part of any one of us is a form we cannot trace with our eyes or grasp with our hands. We are not able to physically feel when the very substance of our eternal being opens with love and hope or begins to cave in on itself with anger and despair. Since we cannot see or touch our inner being, it is sometimes hard to get our minds around its substance and how it grows and withers. We need a way to visualize how life's pressures work on the soul, so we can learn to respond in a way that creates and maintains interior freedom rather than constriction. In *You, Free*, my dear friend Charlotte offers symbols and words to help us begin to feel out the grand space of our interior life and explore the things that are there. The inner being—the very essence of who we are--is always being formed though we may be ignorant of it and fail to realize we have great choice in how we are formed. In this book are the illuminating thoughts and lessons Charlotte shared with me on many afternoons at her cozy kitchen table in years past. I still have many of the scraps of paper on which she drew some of the early forms God was showing her—forms that began to help me as a young woman carve out interior freedom that I yearned for but didn't understand how to make a reality. These images resonated then and now they continue to offer new light. They have been friendly guides to me as I have acted to responsibly form my soul, and I've held these images in my mind's eye while diving into various ancient spiritual practices. On the days when I'm not tending well to my inmost being, I can still see Charlotte's passionate scribbling and once again visualize what is happening within and how I managed to end up in such a space. There are books filled with glorious, life-giving ideas that forever change—in the best way—how we see the world and meet with reality. This is one of those books. Now, read this--and go create your freedom!"

JENNY KNIGHT, CO-AUTHOR OF *THE REFLECTION GUIDE TO BETTER CONVERSATIONS*